The Intimate Journey To Desires

INTIMACY OF GOD

INTIMACY WITH GOD

INTIMACY WITH OTHERS

Dr. Denny Bates

i

"The Intimate Journey To Desires"

Intimacy Of God / Intimacy With God / Intimacy With Others

How To DELIGHT yourself in the Lord and discover your Sweet Spot

By Assessing A Healthy Intimacy In Four Distinctive Ways

(Emotional / Spiritual / Intellectual / Physical)

TABLE OF CONTENTS

Dedication

There is a lot of "life" that takes place on a journey. On a life's journey there can be incredible highs and there can be tragic lows. There are high risks we may take and sometimes, we may even wind up with high rewards. On the other hand, low risk, low rewards. And if we are not careful, low risk-taking, when it comes to our meaningful relationships, will become the norm of a flat line of mediocrity. Because if we do not feel "safe," we are quick to put on a convenient mask of non-intimacy. Walls go up and trusting others goes down. But when trust goes up intimacy goes right along with it. And when intimacy begins to grow, it becomes a beautiful part of the life story.

I'm a firm proponent that People matter, and their Stories matter too. I also have come to believe that intimacy is God's perfect desire for His people. I'm especially moved with gratitude when I observe people who are modeling Biblical intimacy, even when they have had to "fight" for it, after losing it for a while, but regaining it again.

- Who can show the world they are trophies of grace?

- Who can match their walk with their talk?

- Who can show others how to be intimate with God and with each other?

Dennis and Susan Wells are able. This dear couple and their story capsulates why I wrote *The Intimate Journey To Desires*.

As I began to pray through to whom I wanted to dedicate this book, I gave it some time. For each one of my books, I take all my "book dedications" very seriously. I sensed the Lord, with that sweet calm voice, confirm my dedication for this book; it must be the Wells.

It was my privilege and great blessing to be their "matchmaker" years ago. I met Susan when she was only 17 and invited her to be on my ministry team. I met Dennis shortly after and invited him to join my team. We often affectionally called our team, "The God Squad." We traveled in my Red Chevrolet cargo van that had a full-length sofa which faced the side cargo door, "The Holy Ghost Traveling Salvation Van." Little did I realize then, I not only invited them to join my team, but the Lord was putting together an incredible friendship that was formed over 40 years ago and still stands today, stronger than ever.

I was in their wedding. They were in mine. I sang with them. Ministered with them. Went to church with them. Served on the same church staff with them. Traveled the interstate highways and byways with them. Laughed together, cried together, and saw them raise their precious children.

I've seen everything, including their pain.

The ups and downs of ministry.

I saw them fight for their marriage. Almost lose it, only to experience the grace, mercy and forgiveness of God who not only restored their marriage but made it even stronger.

Recently I was with them when they had to tell their middle child a final goodbye.

Why am I sharing all of this? Because I've seen Dennis and Susan become even more intimate with the Lord and with each other. And because of their example, I want you, my treasured reader, to evaluate your own level of intimacy with the Lord and with others.

So, I dedicate *"The Intimate Journey To Desires"* to you, Dennis and Susan. You have always inspired me; always challenged me; but most of all, you have loved me, well.

With all of my love and deepfelt appreciation,

Dr. Denny Bates
September 2022

Acknowledgements

My books are so much better because of those who willingly volunteer their time to read through the sample proof and make sure, first and foremost, that the contents speak to the heart first and then to the mind. They are also people of good grammar and watch out for those pesky typos that get by me, but not them. I am grateful to Bryan Braddock, Marlo Brayboy, Dick Brown, Reeves Cannon, Robby Cisco, Amy Clark, Karen Dixon, Helen Rogers Dobbins, Kimberly Eaker, Laura Harris, Jessica Hayes, Wick Jackson, Kirby King, Myra Leonard, Pam Ludlow, Ron Lyles, Carol Mabe, Traci McCombs, Kim Lanier Medlin, Erika Miller, Debbie and Aubrey Phipps, Katie Stinson Raiford, Lisa Ray, Tamara Rhodes, Sandy Richardson, Leslie Rutten, Patty Smith, Amy Watts, and Leigh Ann Wheeler.

'Every time I think of you, I give thanks to my God. Whenever I pray, I make my requests for all of you with joy, for you have been my partners in spreading the Good News about Christ from the time you first heard it until now. And I am certain that God, who began the good work within you, will continue his work until it is finally finished on the day when Christ Jesus returns.'
Philippians 1:3-6 (NLT)

Preface

got Intimacy?

Real Intimacy?

When I saw the photo image I've chosen for my cover, for me, it was the perfect image when it comes to intimacy.

At the edge of a cliff . . . longing, but oh so careful . . . daring to desire, but will my dreams for a healthy relationship come true . . . with hands on hips . . . trying to see what is in the distance . . . and in the background, there are clouds that fill in the top of the picture . . . but are they clouds that peacefully float in the sky . . . or are they violent storm clouds on the way? Who knows?

There is always a risk when it comes to intimacy. Many will never get to the edge of the cliff. There has been too much heartbreak, betrayal, or severe disappointment in the past. So, they raise the white flag of surrender, settle for less than they deserve, and put up yellow "Caution Tape" around their heart and communicate "Don't get near me" and equally, I'll certainly "not get near you!"

But there are others, the more adventurous, who are "willing to be willing" to climb the mountain and head to the cliff of self-discovery. They want to take action and begin the process, *The Intimate Journey To Desires,* and learn how to use the practical tools for building a healthy intimacy.

This book is for you, just as much as it is for me. For years, I've been on my own personal quest to understand the need for intimacy with God and with others: "How does intimacy work? What does intimacy mean? Why does intimacy matter?" And finally, "Who is intimacy for?" My goal is to address all of those questions in this book but at this time, I'll address the "Who" question first.

The Intimate Journey To Desires is for . . .

- The person who wants to learn about how God is the "gold standard" when it comes to intimacy
- The person who wants to learn how to become more intimate with God
- The person who wants to learn how to grow in an appropriate intimacy who is in a serious dating relationship

The Intimate Journey To Desires is for . . .

- The counselor who is guiding a couple through the process of desiring how to have a biblically based intimate relationship
- The pastor who wants to teach their flock about Biblical intimacy
- The married couple who wants to grow in their own four levels of intimacy: Emotionally, Spiritually, Intellectually, and Physically.

The Intimate Journey To Desires is for . . .

YOU!

Foreword

Denny Bates has been a pastor, mentor, and friend to me for well over two decades and I am a better man for it. You have in your hands another great resource from Denny that is birthed out of not just his study of God's word, but out of his experience with God and His word. Denny writes with wisdom, insight, and care birthed out of his own experiences.

In *The Intimate Journey to Desires,* Denny walks us through the importance and beauty of intimacy with God and how our intimate relationship with the Lord leads us to rich, deep, and vibrant relationships with others. Scripture teaches us to love God and love others and in this insightful and practical book you will be better equipped for this beautiful relational journey with God and others. Denny has lived a life that seeks to know God deeply and I encourage you to take hold of this resource and utilize its teaching to experience the intimacy with God and others that leads to life abundantly.

I pray that as you read this book you will be transformed by a more intimate relationship with Christ.

Reeves Cannon, MA, LPC
Missions Pastor / Executive Pastor, Church at Sandhurst
September 2022

Before we continue . . .

I am fully aware that the intimate journey you are about to experience may be, can I say it, quite daunting for some. I realize that for some of you opening up yourself to any form of intimacy is uncomfortable, to say the least. But I want to commend you now. You've already made great strides. This book is in your hands, but I assure you, my dear reader, you are not taking this journey alone. The Helper, the Counselor, the Teacher, the Comforter, and the Holy Spirit will make this great prayer come alive in your heart:

'When I think of all this, I fall to my knees and pray to the Father, I pray that from his glorious, unlimited resources he will empower you with inner strength through his Spirit. the Creator of everything in heaven and on earth. Then Christ will make his home in your hearts as you trust in him. Your roots will grow down into God's love and keep you strong. And may you have the power to understand, as all God's people should, how wide, how long, how high, and how deep his love is. May you experience the love of Christ, though it is too great to understand fully. Then you will be made complete with all the fullness of life and power that comes from God.' (Ephesians 3:14-19 NLT)

"To . . . be . . . made . . . complete."

That my friend is a wonderful way to describe the goal of Biblical intimacy. Is it really possible? Yes, it is!

'Now all glory to God, who is able, through his mighty power at work within us, to accomplish infinitely more than we might ask or think.' (Ephesians 3:20 NLT).

He is able to empower you to not only begin *The Ultimate Journey To Desires* but to be changed by it.

He is Able!

—

The Intimate Journey To Desires:

How to DELIGHT yourself in the Lord and discover your Sweet Spot

Assessing A Healthy Intimacy In Four Distinctive Ways

(Emotional / Spiritual / Intellectual / Physical)

INTRODUCTION:

Unwrapping the process to having an awareness of knowing and then embracing the desires of your heart is to be your focus. I call it your "Sweet Spot." It is the place where faith, trust and abundant joy intersect in the desires of your heart. Psalm 37:3-5 and Proverbs 3:5-6 will help you DELIGHT yourself in the Lord and discover your Sweet Spot.

'Trust in the Lord and do good; Dwell in the land and cultivate faithfulness. Delight yourself in the Lord; And He will give you the desires of your heart. Commit your way to the Lord, Trust also in Him, and He will do it.' (Psalms 37:3-5 NASB)

'Trust in the Lord with all your heart; do not depend on your own understanding. Seek his will in all you do, and he will show you which path to take.' (Proverbs 3:5-6 NLT)

I've purposefully chosen these two familiar passages of Scripture to better illustrate how much it pleases the Lord to bless you with His very best (the desires of your heart and the clarity we need to choose and then follow His path). All He requires is trust.

- Do you know what desire, what path is best for you? Right now
- Do you know what desire, what path is God's best for you? Right now

Before you even begin to enter the world of intimacy (between you and God and then Emotional, Spiritual, Intellectual, and Physical intimacy with your meaningful relationships), I must ask the question:

What is the *desire* of your heart?

- Have you asked for God to give you His desire, for you?

- For you, in a meaningful relationship if you are single, is your goal to "desire" marriage?

- Or is your desire learning to be content with a healthy singleness? And if you are already married the same principles and need for intimacy applies to you as well.

- Are you sure about any of this?

This is where it is of great importance to TRUST the Lord to do His work in your heart. The word "delight" in this verse means to become like pliable clay. It means not to go into the great promises of this passage of scripture with a preconceived, biased approach. It must be with "open hands, bended knee. Lord, I seek Your will."

Going into this study about the power of intimacy, you need to come with a desire to not only study and learn what God's Word says about intimacy but also be willing to apply what you have learned.

It is my honor to serve as your "tour guide" as I lead you through the three parts of *The Intimate Journey To Desires*. In Part One, you will learn about the "Intimacy Of God" and how He is perfectly intimate within Himself: Father, Son, and Holy Spirit. Part Two will introduce you to how you develop an authentic "Intimacy With God." Finally, Part Three is "Intimacy With Each Other." You are presented with four practical five point assessments for those who desire a healthy perspective of Emotional, Spiritual, Intellectual, and Physical intimacy.

Are you ready to embark on one of the most meaningful journeys you will ever experience? For many, this is the road less traveled. *The Intimate Journey To Your Desires* begins now.

Delight Yourself In The Lord And He Will Give You The Desires Of Your Heart

PART ONE: Intimacy Of God

PART TWO: Intimacy With God

PART THREE: Intimacy With Each Other

Emotional, Spiritual, Intellectual, and Physical assessments

The Intimate Journey To Desires

PART ONE: Intimacy Of God

Intimacy, a noun. (Cambridge Dictionary)

- "Things that are said or done only by people who have a close relationship with each other"

God the Father, God the Son, and God the Holy Spirit are one. They are in perfect harmony, in perfect unity, in perfect intimacy. Why is this so important for you? Because the intimacy OF God is the attractional allure, the unique quality of being both powerfully and mysteriously attractive for you to experience intimacy WITH God.

Father, Son, and Holy Spirit: They are . . .

- Holy

- Merciful and mighty

- Perfect in power, in love and purity

- God in three persons, blessed Trinity

Holy, holy, holy
Lord God almighty
Early in the morning my song shall rise to thee
Holy. holy, holy
Merciful and mighty
God in three persons, blessed Trinity

Holy, holy, holy
All the saints adore Thee
Casting down their golden crowns around the glassy sea
All the cherubim and seraphim are falling down before Thee
Which wert and art and evermore shalt be

Holy, holy, holy
Though the darkness hide Thee
Though the eyes of sinful man Thy glory may not see
Lord, only Thou art holy and there is none beside Thee
Perfect in power, in love and purity

Holy, holy, holy
Lord God almighty
All Thy works shall praise Thy name in earth and sky and sea
Holy, holy, holy
Merciful and mighty

You are God in three persons, blessed Trinity

God is intimate with Himself. Father, Son, Spirit.

'Then God said, "Let us make human beings in our image, to be like us. They will reign over the fish in the sea, the birds in the sky, the livestock, all the wild animals on the earth, and the small animals that scurry along the ground." So God created human beings in his own image. In the image of God he created them; male and female he created them.' (Genesis 1:26-27 NLT)

This passage has much to reveal to us when it comes to the intimate relationship of the Trinity.

First of all, the word "us" is plural. In their own "perfectness" they convened with a Divine agenda that had you and me and the rest of mankind in mind. The Trinity purposed, "let us make human beings in our image, TO BE LIKE US." From His majestic Throne, in this heavenly board room, from this item on the agenda, there was no push back between them, no hostile debate or contention, no split decision. There was unity. There was intimacy.

Throughout the entire Bible the Scriptures declare the unity, the oneness, the sameness, and intimacy of God; the Father, Son, and Holy Spirit. (Read each passage, prayerfully)

'"Listen, O Israel! The Lord is our God, the Lord alone.' (Deuteronomy 6:4 NLT)

'The Father and I are one."' (John 10:30 NLT)

'Jesus came and told his disciples, "I have been given all authority in heaven and on earth. Therefore, go and make disciples of all the nations, baptizing them in the name of the Father and the Son and the Holy Spirit.' (Matthew 28:18-19 NLT)

'But for us, There is one God, the Father, by whom all things were created, and for whom we live. And there is one Lord, Jesus Christ, through whom all things were created, and through whom we live.'
(1 Corinthians 8:6 NLT)

'There are different kinds of spiritual gifts, but the same Spirit is the source of them all. There are different kinds of service, but we serve the same Lord. God works in different ways, but it is the same God who does the work in all of us.' (1 Corinthians 12:4-6 NLT)

'May the grace of the Lord Jesus Christ, the love of God, and the fellowship of the Holy Spirit be with you all.' (2 Corinthians 13:14 NLT)

'As for us, we can't help but thank God for you, dear brothers and sisters loved by the Lord. We are always thankful that God chose you to be among the first to experience salvation—a salvation that came through the Spirit who makes you holy and through your belief in the truth. He called you to salvation when we told you the Good News; now you can share in the glory of our Lord Jesus Christ.'
(2 Thessalonians 2:13-14 NLT)

'For there is one body and one Spirit, just as you have been called to one glorious hope for the future. There is one Lord, one faith, one baptism, one God and Father of all, who is over all, in all, and living through all. '(Ephesians 4:4-6 NLT)

'God the Father knew you and chose you long ago, and his Spirit has made you holy. As a result, you have obeyed him and have been cleansed by the blood of Jesus Christ. May God give you more and more grace and peace.' (1 Peter 1:2 NLT)

'For every child of God defeats this evil world, and we achieve this victory through our faith. And who can win this battle against the world? Only those who believe that Jesus is the Son of God. And Jesus Christ was revealed as God's Son by his baptism in water and by shedding his blood on the cross —not by water only, but by water and blood. And the Spirit, who is truth, confirms it with his testimony.' (1 John 5:4-6 NLT)

'The angel replied, "The Holy Spirit will come upon you, and the power of the Most High will overshadow you. So the baby to be born will be holy, and he will be called the Son of God.' (Luke 1:35 NLT)

'After his baptism, as Jesus came up out of the water, the heavens were opened and he saw the Spirit of God descending like a dove and settling on him. And a voice from heaven said, "This is my dearly loved Son, who brings me great joy."' (Matthew 3:16-17 NLT)

'One day Jesus came from Nazareth in Galilee, and John baptized him in the Jordan River. As Jesus came up out of the water, he saw the heavens splitting apart and the Holy Spirit descending on him like a dove. And a voice from heaven said, "You are my dearly loved Son, and you bring me great joy." The Spirit then compelled Jesus to go into the wilderness, ' (Mark 1:9-12 NLT)

'One day when the crowds were being baptized, Jesus himself was baptized. As he was praying, the heavens opened, and the Holy Spirit, in bodily form, descended on him like a dove. And a voice from heaven said, "You are my dearly loved Son, and you bring me great joy."' (Luke 3:21-22 NLT)

'In the beginning the Word already existed. The Word was with God, and the Word was God. He existed in the beginning with God. God created everything through him, and nothing was created except through him. The Word gave life to everything that was created, and his life brought light to everyone.' (John 1:1-4 NLT)

Second, because there was intimacy The Trinity's creation was perfect, not chaotic. Because of their intimacy, "dreaming the great dreams" were openly discussed among them. Their "blueprints" were perfect. The resources to construct all of creation were limitless. By their word, their unified word that was spoken, a perfect creation appeared out of the chaos. "In the image of God he created them; male and female he created them." This perfect creation is the perfect template for God's purpose: He does His work with males and females. And more than anything, He desires to have an ***intimate relationship*** with His creation, His "image bearers."

'For every house has a builder, but the one who built everything is God.' (Hebrews 3:4 NLT)

'For through him God created everything in the heavenly realms and on earth. He made the things we can see and the things we can't see— such as thrones, kingdoms, rulers, and authorities in the unseen world. Everything was created through him and for him. Christ is the visible image of the invisible God. He existed before anything was created and is supreme over all creation, He existed before anything else, and he holds all creation together.' (Colossians 1:15-17 NLT)

'Long ago God spoke many times and in many ways to our ancestors through the prophets. And now in these final days, he has spoken to us through his Son. God promised everything to the Son as an inheritance, and through the Son he created the universe.' (Hebrews 1:1-2 NLT)

'Lord, there is no one like you! For you are great, and your name is full of power.' (Jeremiah 10:6 NLT)

'When I think of all this, I fall to my knees and pray to the Father, the Creator of everything in heaven and on earth. I pray that from his glorious, unlimited resources he will empower you with inner strength through his Spirit. Then Christ will make his home in your hearts as you trust in him. Your roots will grow down into God's love and keep you strong. And may you have the power to understand, as all God's people should, how wide, how long, how high, and how deep his love is. May you experience the love of Christ, though it is too great to understand fully. Then you will be made complete with all the fullness of life and power that comes from God. Now all glory to God, who is able, through his mighty power at work within us, to accomplish infinitely more than we might ask or think. Glory to him in the church and in Christ Jesus through all generations forever and ever! Amen.' (Ephesians 3:14-21 NLT)

'And this hope will not lead to disappointment. For we know how dearly God loves us, because he has given us the Holy Spirit to fill our hearts with his love. When we were utterly helpless, Christ came at just the right time and died for us sinners.' (Romans 5:5-6 NLT)

'So we have not stopped praying for you since we first heard about you. We ask God to give you complete knowledge of his will and to give you spiritual wisdom and understanding. Then the way you live will always honor and please the Lord, and your lives will produce every kind of good fruit. All the while, you will grow as you learn to know God better and better. We also pray that you will be strengthened with all his glorious power so you will have all the endurance and patience you need. May you be filled with joy, always thanking the Father. He has enabled you to share in the inheritance that belongs to his people, who live in the light. For he has rescued us from the kingdom of darkness and transferred us into the Kingdom of his dear Son, who purchased our freedom and forgave our sins.' (Colossians 1:9-14 NLT)

And finally, this:

'For this is how God loved the world: He gave his one and only Son, so that everyone who believes in him will not perish but have eternal life. God sent his Son into the world not to judge the world, but to save the world through him.' (John 3:16-17 NLT)

Because God is intimate with Himself, He can offer you the deal of a lifetime: Intimacy with Him.

What does that really look like?

Let's begin that wonderful conversation in Part Two: Intimacy With God. Master this and you will never be the same again.

—

The Intimate Journey To Desires:

PART TWO: Intimacy With God

Spiritual growth is not only about coming back into a relationship with God and each other, and about pursuing a pure life, but it is also about coming back to life—the life that God created for people to live. This life of deep relationship, fulfilling work, celebration, and more gives us the life we desire and solves our problems.
~ Henry Cloud and John Townsend ~

but speaking the truth in love,
we are to grow up in all aspects into Him who is the head, even Christ
~ Paul, the Apostle writing to the Disciples of Ephesus (4:15) ~

Good News! There are means available to get you from "here to there" when it comes to spiritual growth (also known as "spiritual formation").

One of the most important aspects of spiritual formation is the "cause and effect" that takes place. I contend that as a believer engages in a growing relationship with God and with others growth will occur. In addition, I am making the case that a disciple who grows in grace, worship, Bible study, prayer, community, service and evangelism will experience measurable spiritual growth.

In God's grace, He has provided various ways of how spiritual growth occurs in the life of the disciple.

Spending time in God's Word, will be a means for change; not just studying it, but reading it, memorizing it, and meditating upon it.

Prayer is another activity that God uses in the disciple's life to be a means for spiritual growth. It is through prayer that the believer is in dialogue with the Maker and Sustainer of the Universe. It is through prayer that the disciple learns to sit in and enjoy His presence. "'Prayer changes things,' people say. It also changes us . . . None of us will keep a life of prayer unless we are prepared to change" (Richard Foster, P*rayer: finding the heart's true home.* 1992, pg. 57)

Obedience is another means to grow spiritually. Cloud and Townsend contribute helpful insights concerning the value of obedience to the disciple. "People who want to experience the true growth revealed in the Bible will shift 180 degrees from the ways of the world to the ways of the kingdom, because only the ways of the kingdom will work (Henry Cloud & John Townsend, *How people grow: what the Bible reveals about personal growth.* 2001, pg. 241). . . . we cannot grow spiritually without obedience. We cannot live apart from God. He is our life" (Cloud & Townsend 2001, pg. 283).

Journaling, writing down one's thoughts and insights, is a helpful tool that can provide spiritual growth. It is important to record the treasures one collects along the way in one's journey. Those special Ebenezers will have great value as one remembers all that the Lord has done (Simon Chan, *Spiritual theology: a systematic theology of the Christian life.* 1998, pg. 156). Embracing one's stewardship of time and self-leadership will become a means to one's spiritual growth. What the disciple chooses to do with their time will have a great impact upon how much spiritual growth will occur. The Christian will either pursue God's Kingdom, or will pour one's life into one's self.

One cannot discount the importance of *the cross* as a means to spiritual growth. The discipled life is a life lived under the shadow of the cross; a cross of sacrifice, pain, suffering, and submission to the will of God.

Being an active member of a spiritual community is also a means to the disciple's spiritual growth. Within the context of community authentic growth occurs both for the individual as well as the group. "Spiritual community, as C. S. Lewis once said, is a good library for discovering God" (Larry Crabb, *The safest place on earth: where people connect and are forever changed.* 1999, pg. 135)

Finally, Richard Foster adds one more unique way of obtaining spiritual growth—there is *the need to also have fun*. "Even the most spiritually advanced—perhaps *especially* the most spiritually advanced—need frequent times of laughter and play and good fun" (Richard Foster, P*rayer: finding the heart's true home.* 1992, pg. 14).

LEARNING HOW TO PRAY GOD'S WORD BY MAKING IT PERSONAL

One of the most fulfilling spiritual disciplines we can do is to pray God's Word back to Him. In a very clear sense, when we are praying God's Word, we are actually praying His will. Praying His Word will increase your faith. Praying His Word is the language of Heaven.

To illustrate I'm going to select a portion of Scripture. Note the brackets [   ] where I insert a more personalized prayer. I'll show you the unedited version first. Then, right below it, the personalized scripture.

Read it outloud. I want YOU to *personalize**** it as you begin to pray God's Word!

From Ephesians 1:2-8 NLT

'May God our Father and the Lord Jesus Christ give you grace and peace.

***'May God [my] Father and the Lord Jesus Christ give [me] grace and peace.

All praise to God, the Father of our Lord Jesus Christ, who has blessed us with every spiritual blessing in the heavenly realms because we are united with Christ.

***All praise to God, the Father of [my] Lord Jesus Christ, who has blessed [me] with every spiritual blessing in the heavenly realms because [I am] united with Christ.

Even before he made the world, God loved us and chose us in Christ to be holy and without fault in his eyes.

***[Lord], Even before [You] made the world, God [You] loved [me] and chose [me] in Christ to be holy and without fault in [your] eyes.

God decided in advance to adopt us into his own family by bringing us to himself through Jesus Christ. This is what he wanted to do, and it gave him great pleasure.

***God [You] decided in advance to adopt [me] into [Your] own family by bringing [me] to Yourself through Jesus Christ. This is what [You] wanted to do [for me], and it gave [You] great pleasure.

So we praise God for the glorious grace he has poured out on us who belong to his dear Son.

***So [I] praise [you] God for the glorious grace [You have] poured out on [me] who [belongs] to [Your] dear Son.

He is so rich in kindness and grace that he purchased our freedom with the blood of his Son and forgave our sins.

***[Lord, You are] so rich in kindness and grace that [You] purchased [my] freedom with the blood of [Your] Son and forgave [all of my] sins.

He has showered his kindness on us, along with all wisdom and understanding. '

***[You have] showered [Your] kindness on [me], along with all wisdom and understanding. '

Got the idea? You have learned how to pray through the entire Bible! The next passage of Scripture is on you. See you in the Secret Place!

'"When you pray, don't be like the hypocrites who love to pray publicly on street corners and in the synagogues where everyone can see them. I tell you the truth, that is all the reward they will ever get. But when you pray, go away by yourself, shut the door behind you, and pray to your Father in private. Then your Father, who sees everything, will reward you.'
(Matthew 6:5-6 NLT)

YOUR ASSESSMENT FOR EXPERIENCING INTIMACY WITH GOD

On a scale of 1 to 5 how would you rate your level of Intimacy when you Worship?

Intimacy in Worship really matters

1	2	3	4	5
Strongly Disagree	Disagree	Somewhat Agree	Agree	Strongly Agree

Other comments:

You are willing to go into a deeper level of Intimacy when you Worship

1	2	3	4	5
Strongly Disagree	Disagree	Somewhat Agree	Agree	Strongly Agree

Other comments:

Intimacy when you Worship usually leaves you edified (built up), uplifted, valued

1	2	3	4	5
Strongly Disagree	Disagree	Somewhat Agree	Agree	Strongly Agree

Other comments:

You often find yourself looking forward to the next opportunity to experience Intimacy when you Worship

1	2	3	4	5
Strongly Disagree	Disagree	Somewhat Agree	Agree	Strongly Agree

Other comments:

You believe Intimacy when you Worship is one of the best paths to achieving God's best for yourself, "Your Sweet Spot."

1	2	3	4	5
Strongly Disagree	Disagree	Somewhat Agree	Agree	Strongly Agree

Other comments:

On a scale of 1 to 5 how would you rate your level of Intimacy when you Pray?

Intimacy when you Pray really matters

1	2	3	4	5
Strongly Disagree	Disagree	Somewhat Agree	Agree	Strongly Agree

Other comments:

You are willing to go into a deeper level of Intimacy when you Pray

1	2	3	4	5
Strongly Disagree	Disagree	Somewhat Agree	Agree	Strongly Agree

Other comments:

Intimacy when you Pray usually leaves you edified (built up), uplifted, valued

1	2	3	4	5
Strongly Disagree	Disagree	Somewhat Agree	Agree	Strongly Agree

Other comments:

You often find yourself looking forward to the next opportunity to experience Intimacy when you Pray

1	2	3	4	5
Strongly Disagree	Disagree	Somewhat Agree	Agree	Strongly Agree

Other comments:

You believe Intimacy when you Pray is one of the best paths to achieving God's best for yourself, "Your Sweet Spot."

1	2	3	4	5
Strongly Disagree	Disagree	Somewhat Agree	Agree	Strongly Agree

Other comments:

On a scale of 1 to 5 how would you rate your level of Intimacy with God's Word?

Intimacy in God's Word really matters

1	2	3	4	5
Strongly Disagree	Disagree	Somewhat Agree	Agree	Strongly Agree

Other comments:

You are willing to go into a deeper level of Intimacy in God's Word

1	2	3	4	5
Strongly Disagree	Disagree	Somewhat Agree	Agree	Strongly Agree

Other comments:

Intimacy in God's Word usually leaves you edified (built up), uplifted, valued

1	2	3	4	5
Strongly Disagree	Disagree	Somewhat Agree	Agree	Strongly Agree

Other comments:

You often find yourself looking forward to the next opportunity to experience Intimacy in God's Word

1	2	3	4	5
Strongly Disagree	Disagree	Somewhat Agree	Agree	Strongly Agree

Other comments:

You believe Intimacy in God's Word is one of the best paths to achieving God's best for yourself, "Your Sweet Spot."

1	2	3	4	5
Strongly Disagree	Disagree	Somewhat Agree	Agree	Strongly Agree

Other comments:

On a scale of 1 to 5 how would you rate your level of Intimacy with The Body of Christ?

Intimacy with The Body of Christ really matters

1	2	3	4	5
Strongly Disagree	Disagree	Somewhat Agree	Agree	Strongly Agree

Other comments:

You are willing to go into a deeper level of Intimacy with The Body of Christ

1	2	3	4	5
Strongly Disagree	Disagree	Somewhat Agree	Agree	Strongly Agree

Other comments:

Intimacy with The Body of Christ usually leaves you edified (built up), uplifted, valued

1	2	3	4	5
Strongly Disagree	Disagree	Somewhat Agree	Agree	Strongly Agree

Other comments:

You often find yourself looking forward to the next opportunity to experience Intimacy with The Body of Christ

1	2	3	4	5
Strongly Disagree	Disagree	Somewhat Agree	Agree	Strongly Agree

Other comments:

You believe Intimacy with The Body of Christ is one of the best paths to achieving God's best for yourself, "Your Sweet Spot."

1	2	3	4	5
Strongly Disagree	Disagree	Somewhat Agree	Agree	Strongly Agree

Other comments:

Great job!

You've read through Part One: Intimacy of God and now Part Two, Intimacy with God.

With that Biblical foundation in place, let's move from the intimacy that is VERTICAL to one that is HORIZONTAL on your intimate journey to desires, Part Three: Intimacy with Each Other.

Now the fun begins!

The Intimate Journey To Desires

God's Best For You! (For Any Meaningful Relationships)

"Don't Settle For Less, Than God's Best!"

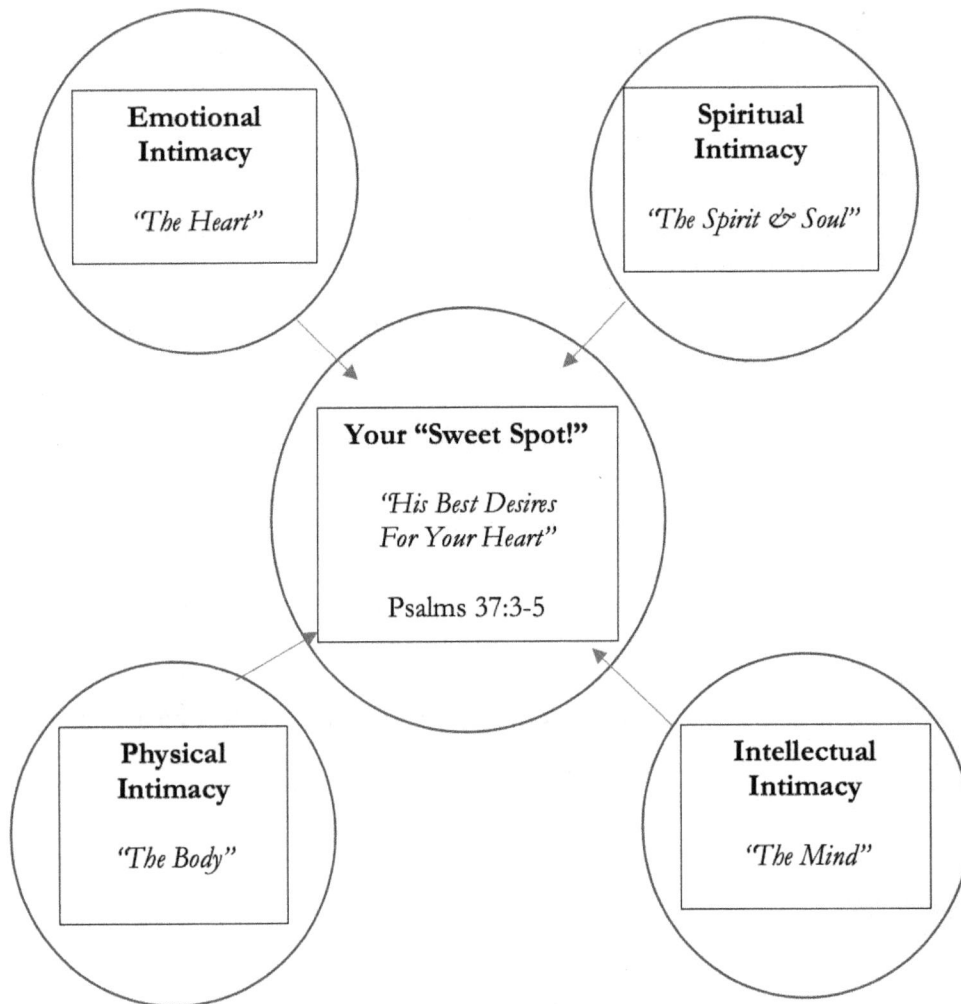

Emotional Intimacy

"The Heart"

Spiritual Intimacy

"The Spirit & Soul"

Your "Sweet Spot!"

"His Best Desires For Your Heart"

Psalms 37:3-5

Physical Intimacy

"The Body"

Intellectual Intimacy

"The Mind"

Intimate Journey To Desires

©2022 Dr. Denny Bates & Something New Ministries

GOD'S BEST FOR YOU!

PART THREE: Intimacy With Others

A Practical Five Point Assessment For Any Meaningful Relationship

Desiring A Healthy Intimacy In Four Essential Ways

"Don't Settle For Less, Than God's Best!"

THIS IS THE GOAL!

>>>This Is Your Sweet Spot<<<

"His Desires For Your Heart"

'Trust in the Lord and do good; Dwell in the land and cultivate faithfulness. Delight yourself in the Lord; And He will give you the desires of your heart. Commit your way to the Lord, Trust also in Him, and He will do it.' (Psalms 37:3-5 NASB)

I am writing this section to the person who wants God's best for them in a meaningful relationship but who is not quite sure what that really means and how to get there. We can become so stuck in a rut where we can't see the Forest because of the Trees. My goal for you and this assessment is to give you a bird's eye view and help you take healthy relationship steps towards your Sweet Spot.

I have chosen this Scripture, Psalms 37:3-5, on purpose. If there is anyone who desires to have an intimate relationship with you, it is Jesus. I'll forgo a deeper Bible study at this time, but I want to share at least a few bullet points of instruction with you to encourage your heart with His timeless promises.

- Trusting in the Lord (at the beginning and end of this passage) are the "bookends" to the Lord giving you the desires of your heart.
- Dwelling in the land and cultivating faithfulness is akin to "abiding, remaining" in the Lord. In other words, you need to stay close to Him as He works in your heart.
- The word "delight" literally means to become like pliable clay where the Potter can form a suitable place in your heart to hold His desires for you.
- Now it gets exciting! He will give you the desires of your heart. But note carefully: these desires are actually His desires for you. It is grace driven and because they not only come from the Lord, it's also His "job" to make His desires, which are now yours, become a reality.
- You have the ability "to close the deal" when you *Commit your way to the Lord, Trust also in Him, and He will do it.'*

Now, like all promises and principles, we can't turn them into a "foolproof formula" for success. Having a relationship with the Lord is about experiencing "intimacy" in a personal relationship with Him. God is not like a slot machine of desire where we keep putting tokens in, waiting to hit the jackpot!

Here is the big test of faith and trust:
- Do I trust Him to give me *His* desires?
- Do I trust Him when *my* desires do not match up with His?
- Will His desires for me disappoint me or do I believe, do I trust, they will eventually bless me?

An intimate God knows exactly what you need as you seek to develop a meaningful and healthy relationship with someone of interest.

I have identified four levels of relational intimacy: Intellectual, Physical, Spiritual, and Emotional. All of them are necessary, in whole, for you to experience God's Best for You. I realize some of this will be uncomfortable. I know. I'm praying for you: take courage. You can do it!

THE DANGERS OF ONLY . . .

Intellectual Intimacy: *"The Mind"* <u>*only*</u> = *Endless days and nights of Trivia Pursuit.*

Intellectual intimacy can include deep and meaningful conversations but the quest for knowledge, and sharing it, for knowledge's sake alone will never hit the Sweet Spot when the other three levels of intimacy are ignored.

'May the words of my mouth and the meditation of my heart be pleasing to you, O Lord, my rock and my redeemer.' (Psalms 19:14 NLT)

On a scale of 1 to 5 how would you rate you and your partner's level of Intellectual Intimacy?

The subjects we talk about really matter

1	2	3	4	5
Strongly Disagree	Disagree	Somewhat Agree	Agree	Strongly Agree

Other comments:

You are more prone to go into a deeper level of conversation than they are

1	2	3	4	5
Strongly Disagree	Disagree	Somewhat Agree	Agree	Strongly Agree

Other comments:

These Intellectual conversations usually leave you edified (built up), uplifted, valued

1	2	3	4	5
Strongly Disagree	Disagree	Somewhat Agree	Agree	Strongly Agree

Other comments:

You often find yourself looking forward to the next round of Intellectual conversations

1	2	3	4	5
Strongly Disagree	Disagree	Somewhat Agree	Agree	Strongly Agree

Other comments:

You believe Intellectual Intimacy is one of the best paths to achieving God's best for yourself

1	2	3	4	5
Strongly Disagree	Disagree	Somewhat Agree	Agree	Strongly Agree

Other comments:

Physical Intimacy: *"The Body" <u>only</u> = A never-ending, unfulfilling, lacking real satisfaction.*

True, Physical Intimacy can "be good for a season," but will always lead to a non-productive treadmill, preventing you from ever reaching your Sweet Spot if that is all you are working on. Physical Intimacy "only" is a fraud as it seeks to become your Sweet Spot but in reality, it will end up causing a relationship to sour if the three other areas of intimacy are shunned.

This should be the final area of intimacy to reach your Sweet Spot.

'Run from sexual sin! No other sin so clearly affects the body as this one does. For sexual immorality is a sin against your own body. Don't you realize that your body is the temple of the Holy Spirit, who lives in you and was given to you by God? You do not belong to yourself, for God bought you with a high price. So you must honor God with your body.'
(1 Corinthians 6:18-20 NLT).

On a scale of 1 to 5 how would you rate you and your partner's level of Physical Intimacy?

Physical touch really matters

1	2	3	4	5
Strongly Disagree	Disagree	Somewhat Agree	Agree	Strongly Agree

Other comments:

You are more willing to go into a deeper level of Physical Intimacy than they are

1	2	3	4	5
Strongly Disagree	Disagree	Somewhat Agree	Agree	Strongly Agree

Other comments:

Physical Intimacy usually leaves you edified (built up), uplifted, valued

1	2	3	4	5
Strongly Disagree	Disagree	Somewhat Agree	Agree	Strongly Agree

Other comments:

You often find yourself looking forward to the next round of Physical Intimacy

1	2	3	4	5
Strongly Disagree	Disagree	Somewhat Agree	Agree	Strongly Agree

Other comments:

You believe Physical Intimacy is one of the best paths to achieving God's best for yourself

1	2	3	4	5
Strongly Disagree	Disagree	Somewhat Agree	Agree	Strongly Agree

Other comments:

Note a final word of caution: Even when Intellectual Intimacy is paired with Physical Intimacy, God's best for you with His Desires He has placed in your heart **will never** be achieved because,

THERE ARE TWO ADDITIONAL LEVELS OF INTIMACY THAT HAVE TO BE ACHIEVED TO REACH YOUR SWEET SPOT

Spiritual Intimacy: *"The Spirit and Soul"* = *A supernatural bond that will hold people together when everything seeks to pull them apart.*

Spiritual growth that occurs within the context of meaningful relationships means that "iron sharpens iron." Faith is forged by His Word and by prayer. Reading The Bible and Praying The Word together is one of the most intimate experiences that can occur in a relationship. It's not quite like heaven, but it sure is close as you breathe in heaven's air.

'Let your roots grow down into him, and let your lives be built on him. Then your faith will grow strong in the truth you were taught, and you will overflow with thankfulness.' (Colossians 2:7 NLT)

'May God give you more and more grace and peace as you grow in your knowledge of God and Jesus our Lord.' (2 Peter 1:2 NLT)

On a scale of 1 to 5 how would you rate you and your partner's level of Spiritual Intimacy?

We frequently study God's Word and Pray together

1	2	3	4	5
Strongly Disagree	Disagree	Somewhat Agree	Agree	Strongly Agree

Other comments:

You are more willing to go into a deeper level of Spiritual Intimacy than they are

1	2	3	4	5
Strongly Disagree	Disagree	Somewhat Agree	Agree	Strongly Agree

Other comments:

Spiritual Intimacy usually leaves you edified (built up), uplifted, valued

1	2	3	4	5
Strongly Disagree	Disagree	Somewhat Agree	Agree	Strongly Agree

Other comments:

You often find yourself looking forward to the next opportunity for Spiritual Intimacy

1	2	3	4	5
Strongly Disagree	Disagree	Somewhat Agree	Agree	Strongly Agree

Other comments:

You believe Spiritual Intimacy is one of the best paths to achieving God's best for yourself

1	2	3	4	5
Strongly Disagree	Disagree	Somewhat Agree	Agree	Strongly Agree

Other comments:

Emotional Intimacy: *"The Heart"* = *Herein lies the path where trust and feeling safe and the need to be needed comes alive.*

Perhaps, this level of intimacy may be the most significant one of all four: the need to feel safe in a relationship. The need to be needed and cherished is an essential desire that must not be quenched. Why? Because Emotional Intimacy is the place where true transparency exists, where you are free to "be." Emotional Intimacy is where you become "naked."

''I am my beloved's, And his desire is for me.' (Song of Solomon 7:10 NASB)

To gain a more concise meaning of these terms like "feeling safe," "the need to be needed," and "cherished," here are a few thoughtful suggestions:

Feeling Safe: Safe from rejection. Safe from a judgmental or critical spirit. Safe from being misunderstood. Safe to let your guard down. Safe "to just be." Safe.

The Need to be Needed: To be desired. To be included. To believe without your presence, your absence is apparent.

Cherished: I matter. I'm valued. I'm important. I count. I'm known. I'm understood. I'm heard. The obvious—I'm loved.

On a scale of 1 to 5 how would you rate you and your partner's level of Emotional Intimacy?

Emotional Intimacy really matters

1	2	3	4	5
Strongly Disagree	Disagree	Somewhat Agree	Agree	Strongly Agree

Other comments:

You are more willing to go into a deeper level of Emotional Intimacy than they are

1	2	3	4	5
Strongly Disagree	Disagree	Somewhat Agree	Agree	Strongly Agree

Other comments:

Emotional Intimacy usually leaves you edified (built up), uplifted, valued

1	2	3	4	5
Strongly Disagree	Disagree	Somewhat Agree	Agree	Strongly Agree

Other comments:

You often find yourself looking forward to the next opportunity to experience Emotional Intimacy

1	2	3	4	5
Strongly Disagree	Disagree	Somewhat Agree	Agree	Strongly Agree

Other comments:

You believe Emotional Intimacy is one of the best paths to achieving God's best for yourself

1	2	3	4	5
Strongly Disagree	Disagree	Somewhat Agree	Agree	Strongly Agree

Other comments:

THE SUMMARY OF THE FOUR LEVELS OF INTIMACY AND YOUR NEXT STEPS TO REACH YOUR SWEET SPOT

With any relationship you are in, God wants you to live in wholeness. There is great value in each one of these levels of intimacy. The goal for you is to experience intimate relationships like a well-oiled machine. Each one, on its own is insufficient. It requires all four: Intellectual Intimacy, Physical Intimacy, Spiritual Intimacy, and Emotional Intimacy. I suppose the question is this: Is there a right sequence that begins the process? Where one begins is where one ends. Every relationship is different, but this is how I see things.

For me, it begins with Emotional Intimacy. Without this, the other three levels will be quenched from reaching their most optimum expression. Remember, go back to what Emotional Intimacy is:

Emotional Intimacy: *"The Heart"* = *Herein lies the path where trust, feeling safe, and the need to be needed comes alive.*

No safety? No way. No safety? No peace. No safety? It may be God's way of leading you to look elsewhere in pursuing the right kind of person who will partner with you in your quest to live in your Sweet Spot.

But if there is Emotional Intimacy then I see the following sequence:

Emotional Intimacy (because you trust)

    leads to Spiritual Intimacy (because you grow)

        which leads to Intellectual Intimacy (because you learn)

            which will finally lead to Physical Intimacy (because you love)

If any of these are out of order, I believe you will be frustrated even at the risk of not settling for God's Best!

But that is my idea, for what it's worth. Where you begin may not matter to you. What is crucial is that over time, all four levels of intimacy must be achieved if you want to experience God's Best for You, your Sweet Spot.

If you achieve one level of Intimacy and go no further, then rest in that experience, but be assured, you'll most likely never come to your Sweet Spot. Two out of four? An average relationship, at best. Three levels of experiencing intimacy, you are getting there. But again, so close but so far away. But those who are willing to not settle for less and get God's best, you will never regret it.

My final word for you? Trust the Process. Just get started.

Now it's time to "keep score" on how you responded to the four assessments. I believe we should keep score on the things that matter. Go back to each assessment and post your total scores for each one. Then I'll ask you respond to three final statements:

Your greatest challenge with this level of Intimacy so far has been . . .

Based on this challenge, The First Thing You Need To Do is . . .

Three of your most important life lessons you learned because of (Intellectual, Physical, Spiritual, Emotional) Intimacy

Now, for the bottom line:

>>>On the next page, Total your Score From

The Five Statements Of Each Level Of Intimacy<<<

Intellectual Intimacy: Total Score _____

1	2	3	4	5
Strongly Disagree	Disagree	Somewhat Agree	Agree	Strongly Agree

21 to 25 = Elevated Living!

16 to 20 = Charging Ahead!

11 to 15 = Almost There!

6 to 10 = Ready To Change!

1 to 5 = Something Needs To Change!

Your greatest challenge with Intellectual Intimacy so far has been . . .

Based on this challenge, The First Thing You Need To Do is . . .

Three of your most important life lessons you learned because of Intellectual Intimacy

Physical Intimacy: Total Score _____

1	2	3	4	5
Strongly Disagree	Disagree	Somewhat Agree	Agree	Strongly Agree

21 to 25 = Elevated Living!

16 to 20 = Charging Ahead!

11 to 15 = Almost There!

6 to 10 = Ready To Change!

1 to 5 = Something Needs To Change!

Your greatest challenge with Physical Intimacy so far has been . . .

Based on this challenge, The First Thing You Need To Do is . . .

Three of your most important life lessons you learned because of Physical Intimacy

Spiritual Intimacy: Total Score _____

1	2	3	4	5
Strongly Disagree	Disagree	Somewhat Agree	Agree	Strongly Agree

21 to 25 = Elevated Living!

16 to 20 = Charging Ahead!

11 to 15 = Almost There!

6 to 10 = Ready To Change!

1 to 5 = Something Needs To Change!

Your greatest challenge with Spiritual Intimacy so far has been . . .

Based on this challenge, The First Thing You Need To Do is . . .

Three of your most important life lessons you learned because of Intellectual Intimacy

Emotional Intimacy: Total Score _____

1	2	3	4	5
Strongly Disagree	Disagree	Somewhat Agree	Agree	Strongly Agree

21 to 25 = Elevated Living!

16 to 20 = Charging Ahead!

11 to 15 = Almost There!

6 to 10 = Ready To Change!

1 to 5 = Something Needs To Change!

Your greatest challenge with Emotional Intimacy so far has been . . .

Based on this challenge, The First Thing You Need To Do is . . .

Three of your most important life lessons you learned because of Emotional Intimacy

Addendum:

Some Final Thoughts After Learning About
Intimacy OF God, Intimacy WITH God, and Intimacy WITH Each Other

Congratulations for taking the road less traveled on your intimate journey to desires!

One of my goals has been to introduce you, perhaps in a fresh way, to the intimacy of God. Far more study is required to fully grasp the incredible doctrine of The Trinity, but I wanted to at least begin the conversation with you about what "Perfect Intimacy" looks like from our view.

Another goal was to show you through some practical examples of what intimacy with God will accomplish for your life. I mentioned previously if you can master this, it will change your life.

Finally, my remaining goal has been to make you think about the choices you make when it comes to intimacy with others. Though no survey or assessment is perfect in concept, I do believe the system I shared with you will be useful to both you and to the other meaningful relationship you are pursuing.

Adding up the "scores" is one thing. Being able to share them and then interpret your discoveries together is an even greater level of intimacy that requires much grace, sharp friends, and lots of encouragement!

'Three different times I begged the Lord to take it away. Each time he said, "My grace is all you need. My power works best in weakness." So now I am glad to boast about my weaknesses, so that the power of Christ can work through me. That's why I take pleasure in my weaknesses, and in the insults, hardships, persecutions, and troubles that I suffer for Christ. For when I am weak, then I am strong.' (2 Corinthians 12:8-10 NLT)

'As iron sharpens iron, so a friend sharpens a friend.' (Proverbs 27:17 NLT)

'So encourage each other and build each other up, just as you are already doing.' (1 Thessalonians 5:11 NLT)

The Assessments

SCORES OF EACH ASSESSMENT (out of a possible 100):

Intellectual: _____

Physical: _____

Spiritual: _____

Emotional: _____

TOTAL SCORE: _____

Scale of Interpretation for Total Score

91 to 100 = You Are Living In Your Sweet Spot!

61 to 90 = Don't Stop Growing Now!

41 to 60 = Almost There!

21 to 40 = Time For Some Changes!

5 to 20 = Adjust And Go!

Afterword

A Primer On How You Can Grow By Increasing Your Level Of Intimacy

INTELLECTUAL Intimacy:

Read, Read, Read. Listen, Listen, Listen. Think, Think, Think. Then . . . Talk.

PHYSICAL Intimacy:

Don't Push. Be Patient. Don't Pressure. Be Protective

SPIRITUAL Intimacy:

Go to the Word. Stay in the Word. Pray the Word. Live the Word. Share the Word.

EMOTIONAL Intimacy:

Protect your Heart. Protect your Mind. Project Wholeness. Rinse and Repeat.

Feeling Safe Matters. Your Story Matters. You Matter. Rinse and Repeat.

Trust the Lord:

Trust the Lord with all your Desires. Rinse and Repeat.

'Trust in the Lord and do good; Dwell in the land and cultivate faithfulness. Delight yourself in the Lord; And He will give you the desires of your heart. Commit your way to the Lord, Trust also in Him, and He will do it.' (Psalms 37:3-5 NASB)

Trust the Lord with all your Heart and trust Him that He knows the best PATH for you. Rinse and Repeat.

'Trust in the Lord with all your heart; do not depend on your own understanding. Seek his will in all you do, and he will show you which path to take.' (Proverbs 3:5-6 NLT)

SUBJECT INDEX

An Introduction to the Subject Index for
The Intimate Journey To Desires:

Years ago, I had a friend share with me that a good book can become a great book if it has a useful subject index. I agree with him. What is provided for you in the coming pages is a comprehensive subject index that covers how to experience the timeless principles from *The Intimate Journey To Desires*. This book is much more than a book of helpful information. It is treasure trove of inspirational thoughts and never-ending starting points for a dynamic personal and small group Bible study.

How to use this valuable resource:

You can use this index as a Bible Study on a topic that you want to become more familiar with in your search for spiritual growth. For example, you may wish to study the topic of **Create—Creator—Creation.**

Create—Creator—Creation.
> Fact.
>> Every house has a builder, but the one who built everything is God. Pg. 5
>> God created all things. Pg. 4
> Jesus holds all creation together. Pg. 5
> God created everything through Jesus, and nothing was created except through him. The Word gave life to everything that was created. Pg. 5
> The Father, the Creator of everything in heaven and on earth. Pg. 6
> Through the Son God created the universe. Pg. 6

See how it works? In this illustration, you have been shown at least six Bible study points based upon the topic of Create—Creator—Creation. There are more subjects in this comprehensive study resource that will provide you many years of enriching times of study, reflection, and personal growth.

A
Able.
> God is able. Pg. 6

Adopt.
> Promise.
>> God decided in advance to adopt us into his own family by bringing us to himself through Jesus Christ. This is what he wanted to do, and it gave him great pleasure. Pg. 9

B
Baptism—Baptize.
> Duty.
>> Baptize disciples of all nations. Pg. 4
> Of Jesus. Pg. 5
> One Baptism. Pg. 4

Belief—Believe.
> Promise.
> > He gave his one and only Son, so that everyone who believes in him will not perish but have eternal life. Pg. 6

Blood.
> Cleansed by the blood of Jesus Christ. Pg. 5
> Promise.
> > He is so rich in kindness and grace that he purchased our freedom with the blood of his Son and forgave our sins. Pg. 10

Body.
> Fact.
> > Your body is the temple of the Holy Spirit, who lives in you and was given to you by God. You do not belong to yourself, for God bought you with a high price. So you must honor God with your body. Pg. 21

Body of Christ.
> Intimacy with the Body of Christ really matters. Pg. 16
> Results of having a deeper level of intimacy with the Body of Christ. Pg. 16, 17

C
Chan, Simon. Quote of. Pg. 7

Cloud, Henry. Quote of. Pg. 7

Commit.
> Your way to the Lord. Pg. 1, 19

Crab, Larry. Quote of. Pg. 8

Create—Creator—Creation.
> Fact.
> > Every house has a builder, but the one who built everything is God. Pg. 5
> > God created all things. Pg. 4
> Jesus holds all creation together. Pg. 5
> God created everything through Jesus, and nothing was created except through him. The Word gave life to everything that was created. Pg. 5
> The Father, the Creator of everything in heaven and on earth. Pg. 6
> Through the Son God created the universe. Pg. 6

D
Dark—Darkness.
> Fact.
> > He has rescued us from the kingdom of darkness and transferred us into the Kingdom of his dear Son, who purchased our freedom and forgave our sins. Pg. 6

Delight.
> Meaning of. Pg. 1, 19
> Yourself in the Lord. Pg. 1

Friend—Friendship.

Fact.

As iron sharpens iron, so a friend sharpens a friend. Pg. 33

G
God.

Even before he made the world, God loved us and chose us in Christ to be holy and without fault in his eyes. Pg. 9

Every house has a builder, but the one who built everything is God. Pg. 5

God created everything through Jesus, and nothing was created except through him. The Word gave life to everything that was created. Pg. 5

God decided in advance to adopt us into his own family by bringing us to himself through Jesus Christ. This is what he wanted to do, and it gave him great pleasure. Pg. 9

God; Father, Son, Holy Spirit are in perfect harmony, in perfect unity, in perfect intimacy. Pg. 3

Fact. God is intimate with Himself. Father, Son, Spirit. Pg. 4

Oneness of. Pg. 4

Promise.

Your roots will grow down into God's love and keep you strong. Pg. 6

Sameness of. Pg. 4

Unity of. Pg. 4

Grace.

Is all you need. Pg. 33

Kind of.

Glorious. Pg. 9

Promise.

He is so rich in kindness and grace that he purchased our freedom with the blood of his Son and forgave our sins. Pg. 10

May God give you more and more grace and peace. Pg. 5, 23

May God our Father and the Lord Jesus Christ give you grace and peace. Pg. 9

H
Helpless.

Fact.

When we were utterly helpless, Christ came at just the right time and died for us sinners. Pg. 6

Hope.

Does not lead to disappointment. Pg. 6

Holy.

Fact.

God is holy. Pg. 3

Lyrics to Holy, Holy, Holy. Pg. 3, 4

His Spirit has made you holy. Pg. 5

House.

Fact.

Every house has a builder, but the one who built everything is God. Pg. 5

Jesus (continued).

Through the Son God created the universe. Pg. 6

Judge—Judgement.

Fact.

God sent his Son into the world not to judge the world, but to save the world through him. Pg. 6

K
Kind—Kindness.

Promise.

He is so rich in kindness and grace that he purchased our freedom with the blood of his Son and forgave our sins. Pg. 10

He has showered his kindness on us, along with all wisdom and understanding. Pg. 10

Kingdom.

Fact.

He has rescued us from the kingdom of darkness and transferred us into the Kingdom of his dear Son, who purchased our freedom and forgave our sins. Pg. 6

L
Love.

Promise.

May you experience the love of Christ, though it is too great to understand fully. Pg. 6

May you have the power to understand, as all God's people should, how wide, how long, how high, and how deep his love is. Pg. 6

Your roots will grow down into God's love and keep you strong. Pg. 6

M
Meditate—Meditation.

May the words of my mouth and the meditation of my heart be pleasing to you, O Lord, my rock and my redeemer. Pg. 20

N
Name of the Lord.

Is full of power. Pg. 6

O
One.

Fact. The Father and Jesus are one. Pg. 4

P
Path.

Promise.

He will show you which path to take. Pg.1, 35

Peace.

Promise.

May God give you more and more grace and peace. Pg. 5, 23

Peace (continued).

        May God our Father and the Lord Jesus Christ give you grace and peace. Pg. 9

Please—Pleasing.

        May the words of my mouth and the meditation of my heart be pleasing to you, O Lord,
                my rock and my redeemer. Pg. 20

Prayer.

        Example of praying God's Word. Pg. 6
        Kind of.
                Persistence in prayer. Pg. 6
        Intimacy in Prayer really matters. Pg. 12
        Instructions on how to pray. Pg. 10
        Learning how to pray God's Word by making it personal. Pg. 9
        Prayer request.
                May you be filled with joy, always thanking the Father. Pg. 6
                May the words of my mouth and the meditation of my heart be pleasing to you, O Lord,
                        my rock and my redeemer. Pg. 20
                The way you live will always honor and please the Lord. Pg. 6
                We ask God to give you complete knowledge of his will and to give you spiritual wisdom
                        and understanding. Pg. 6
                You will be strengthened with all his glorious power so you will have all the endurance
                and patience you need. Pg. 6
                You will grow as you learn to know God better and better. Pg. 6
                Your life will produce every kind of good fruit. Pg. 6
        Results of intimacy in Prayer. Pg. 13,14

R
Relationship.

        Fact.
                An intimate God knows exactly what you need as you seek to live in your Sweet Spot
                        when it comes to developing a meaningful and healthy relationship with
                        someone of interest. Pg. 20
                With any relationship you are in, God wants you to live in wholeness. Pg. 27
        Having a relationship with the Lord is about experiencing "intimacy" in a personal relationship
                with Him. Pg. 19

Redeem—Redeemer.

        May the words of my mouth and the meditation of my heart be pleasing to you, O Lord,
                my rock and my redeemer. Pg. 20

Rescue—Rescued.

        Fact.
                He has rescued us from the kingdom of darkness and transferred us into the Kingdom
                of his dear Son, who purchased our freedom and forgave our sins. Pg. 6

Resources.

        Kind of.
                Unlimited. Pg. 6

U
Understand—Understanding.

Promise.

He has showered his kindness on us, along with all wisdom and understanding. Pg. 10

Warning.

Do not depend on your own understanding. Pg. 1, 35

W
Weak—Weakness.

Fact.

His power works best in your weakness. Pg. 33

Wilderness.

Of Jesus.

The Spirit compelled Jesus to go into the wilderness. Pg. 5

Will.

Duty.

Seek his will in all you do. Pg. 1, 35

Words.

May the words of my mouth and the meditation of my heart be pleasing to you, O Lord, my rock and my redeemer. Pg. 20

Wisdom.

Promise.

He has showered his kindness on us, along with all wisdom and understanding. Pg. 10

Word of God.

Intimacy in God's Word really matters. Pg. 14

Jesus is the Word of God. Pg. 5

Results of having an intimate experience in God's Word. Pg. 14, 15

Worship.

Intimacy in Worship really matters. Pg. 11

Results of intimate Worship. Pg. 11, 12

SCRIPTURE INDEX

God's Word is the focal point mentioned in this book. We believe we have far surpassed our goal with this Scripture index where there are forty different passages of Scripture (and some are used more than once) with noted page numbers for easy reference.

"The whole counsel of God, concerning all things necessary for his own glory, man's salvation, faith, and life, is either expressly set down in scripture, or by good and necessary consequence may be deduced from scripture: unto which nothing at any time is to be added, whether by new revelations of the Spirit, or traditions of men." —Westminster Confession of Faith

~ Sola Scriptura ~

Topical Bibliography for the Quality Disciple

Spiritual Disciplines

1. Foster, Richard. 1988. *Celebration of discipline: the path to spiritual growth.* San Francisco, CA: Harper San Francisco.

2. Willard, Dallas. 1988. *The spirit of the disciplines: understanding how God changes lives.* San Francisco, CA: Harper San Francisco.

Prayer

3. Foster, Richard. 1992. P*rayer: Finding the Heart's True Home.* San Francisco, CA: Harper San Francisco.

4. Lockyer, Herbert. 1959. *All the prayers of the Bible.* Grand Rapids, MI: Zondervan.

5. Murray, Andrew. 1983, reprint. *Living a prayerful life.* Minneapolis, MN: Bethany House.

6. Duewel, Wesley L. 1986. *Touch the world through prayer.* Grand Rapids, MI: Francis Asbury Press.

7. Bounds, E. M. 2004. *The complete works of E. M. Bounds on prayer.* Grand Rapids, MI: Baker Books.

8. Sanders, J. Oswald. 1980. *Spiritual leadership.* Chicago, IL: Moody Press.

Bible Study

9. McKnight, Scot. 2008. *The blue parakeet: rethinking how you read the Bible.* Grand Rapids, MI: Zondervan.

10. McQuilkin, Robertson. 1992. *Understanding and applying the Bible,* Chicago, IL: Moody Press.

11. Peterson, Eugene H. 2006. *Eat this book: a conversation in the art of spiritual reading.* Grand Rapids, MI: Wm. B. Eerdmans Publishing Co.

Worship

12. MacDonald, James. 2006. *Downpour.* Nashville, TN: Broadman & Holdman.

13. Thomas, Gary. 2000. *Sacred Pathways: discover your soul's path to God, first Zondervan edition.* Grand Rapids, MI: Zondervan.

Grace

14. Strombeck, J. F. 1947, (2nd edition). *Disciplined by grace: studies in Christian conduct.* Moline, IL. Strombeck Agency, Inc; distributed by Van Kampen Press, Chicago, IL.

15. Swindoll, Charles, R. 2003. *The Grace Awakening.* Nashville, TN: W Publishing Group.

Community

16. Bates, Denny. 2005. *Building a Christian community of friends.* Florence, SC: Something New Christian Publishers.

17. Crabb, Larry. 1999. *The safest place on earth: where people connect and are forever changed.* Nashville, TN: Word Publishing.

Service

18. Rees, Erik. 2006. *S.H.A.P.E.: finding and fulfilling your unique purpose for life.* Grand Rapids, MI: Zondervan.

Evangelism

19. Coleman, Robert E. 1963, 1964, 1993. [New Spire edition 1994]. *The master plan of evangelism.* Grand Rapids, MI: Fleming H. Revell.

20. McQuilkin, Robertson. 1984, 2002 (rev). *The great omission.* Waynesboro, GA: Authentic Media.

21. Pippert, Rebecca Manley. 1979. *Out of the salt shaker and into the world.* Downers Grove, IL: InterVarsity Press.

Discipleship and the Christian Life

22. Allender, Dan B. 2006. *Leading with a limp: turning your struggles into strengths.* Colorado Springs, CO: Waterbrook Press.

23. Anderson, Keith R. and Reese, Randy D. 1999. *Spiritual mentoring: a guide for seeking and giving direction.* Downers Grove, IL: InterVarsity Press.

24. Arn, Win and Charles. 1998. *The master's plan for making disciples, 2nd edition.* Grand Rapids, MI: Baker Books.

25. Barna, George. 2001. *Growing true disciples: new strategies for producing genuine followers of Christ.* Colorado Springs, CO: Waterbrook Press.

26. Biehl, Bobb. 1996. *Mentoring: confidence in finding a mentor and becoming one.* Nashville, TN: Broadman and Holman Publishers.

27. Blackaby, Henry and Richard. 2001. *Spiritual leadership: moving people to God's agenda.* Nashville, TN: Broadman & Holman Publishers.

28. Boa, Kenneth. 2006. *The perfect leader: practicing the leadership traits of God.* Colorado Springs, CO: Victor (Cook Communications Ministries).

29. Burchett, Harold E. 1980. *Spiritual Life Studies.* Published by the author.

30. Campbell, James R. 2009. *Mentor like Jesus.* Nashville, TN: B & H Publishing Group.

31. Chambers, Oswald. 1985. *Christian disciplines: volumes 1 and 2*. Grand Rapids, MI: Chosen Books.

32. Chan, Simon. 1998. *Spiritual theology: a systematic theology of the Christian life*. Downers Grove, IL: InterVarsity Press.

33. Clinton, J. Robert and Richard W. 1991. *The mentor handbook*. Altadena, CA: Barnabas Publishers.

34. Cloud, Henry and Townsend, John. 2001. *How people grow: what the Bible reveals about personal growth*. Grand Rapids, MI: Zondervan.

35. Coleman, Robert E. 1987. *The Master Plan of Discipleship*. Old Tappan, NJ: Fleming H. Revell.

36. Hagberg, Janet O., and Guelich, Robert A. 2005, 1995. *The critical journey: stages in the life of faith*. Salem, WI: Sheffield Publishing Company.

37. Hanks, Billie Jr., and Shell, William A. 1982. *Discipleship: the best writings from the most experienced disciplemakers*. Grand Rapids, MI: The Zondervan Corporation.

38. Harney, Kevin. 2007. *Leadership from the inside out: examining the inner life of a healthy church leader*. Grand Rapids, MI: Zondervan.

39. Hart, Arcihbald D. 1995. *Adrenaline and Stress*. Nashville, TN: W. Publishing Group.

40. Hawkins, Greg L., Parkinson, Cally, and Arnson, Eric. 2007. *Reveal*. Barrington, IL: Willow Creek Resources.

41. Hawkins, Greg L. and Parkinson, Cally. 2008. *Follow me*. Barrington, IL: Willow Creek Resources.

42. Hendricks, Howard and William. 1995. *As iron sharpens iron*. Chicago, IL: Moody Publishers.

43. Hettinga, Jan David. 1996. *Follow me: experience the loving leadership of Jesus*. Colorado Springs, CO: NavPress.

44. Hull, Bill. 2004. *Choose the life: exploring a faith that embraces discipleship*. Grand Rapids, MI: Baker Books.

45. Hull, Bill. 1990. *The disciple-making church*. Grand Rapids, MI: Fleming H. Revell.

46. Hull, Bill. 1995. *Building high commitment in a low commitment world*. Grand Rapids, MI: Fleming H. Revell.

47. Hull, Robert W. 2006. *The complete book of discipleship*. Colorado Springs, NavPress.

48. Ingram, Chip. 2007. *Good to great in God's eyes: 10 practices great Christians have in common*. Grand Rapids, MI: Baker Books.

49. Lovelace, Richard J. 1985. *Renewal as a way of life: a guidebook for spiritual growth*. Downers Grove, IL: InterVarsity Press.

50. MacArthur, John F. Jr. 1976. *Keys to spiritual growth*. Old Tappan, NJ: Fleming H. Revell Company.

51. Mancini, Will. 2008. *Church unique: how missional leaders cast vision, capture culture, and create movement*. San Francisco, CA: Jossey-Bass.

52. Maxwell, John C. 2005. *The 360-degree leader: developing your influence from anywhere in the organization.* Nashville, TN: Thomas Nelson, Inc.

53. McCallum, Dennis and Lowery, Jessica. 2006. *Organic disciplemaking: mentoring others into spiritual maturity and leadership.* Houston, TX: Touch Publications.

54. McIntosh, Gary L. and Rima, Samuel D., Sr. 1997. *Overcoming the dark side of leadership: the paradox of personal dysfunction.* Grand Rapids, MI: Baker Books.

55. Morley, Patrick, David Delk, and Brett Clemmer. 2006. *No man left behind: how to build a thriving disciple-making ministry for every man in your church.* Chicago, IL: Moody Publishers.

56. Nouwen, Henri J. M. 1975. *Reaching Out: the three movements of the spiritual life.* Garden City, NY: Doubleday and Company, Inc.

57. Ogden, Greg. 2003. *Transforming discipleship: making disciples a few at a time.* Downers Grove, IL: InterVarsity Press.

58. Olson, David T. 2008. *The American church in crisis.* Grand Rapids, MI: Zondervan.

59. Peterson, Jim. 1993. *Lifestyle discipleship: the challenge of following Jesus in today's world.* Colorado Springs, CO: NavPress.

60. Pue, Carson. 2005. *Mentoring leaders: wisdom for developing character, calling, and competency.* Grand Rapids, MI: Baker Books.

61. Putnam, David. 2008. *Breaking the discipleship code.* Nashville, TN: B&H Publishing Group.

62. Sanders, J. Oswald. (1994). *Spiritual discipleship.* Chicago, IL: Moody Publishers.

63. Scazzero, Peter L. (2003). *The emotionally healthy church: a strategy for discipleship that actually changes lives.* Grand Rapids, MI: Zondervan.

64. Stanford, Miles J. 1982. *The green letters: principles of spiritual growth.* Grand Rapids, MI: Zondervan Publishing House.

65. Stanley, Paul D. and Clinton, Robert J. 1992. *Connecting: the mentoring relationships you need to succeed in life.* Colorado Springs, CO: NavPress.

66. Waggoner, Brad J. 2008. *The shape of faith to come: spiritual formation and the future of discipleship.* Nashville, TN: B&H Publishing Group.

67. Willard, Dallas. 1998. *The divine conspiracy: rediscovering our hidden life in God.* San Francisco, CA: HarperSanFrancisco.

68. Willard, Dallas. 2006. *The great omission: reclaiming Jesus's essential teachings on discipleship.* San Francisco, CA: HarperSanFrancisco.

69. Warren, Rick. 1995. *The purpose-driven church.* Grand Rapids, MI: Zondervan Publishing House.

70. Warren, Rick. 2002. *The purpose-driven life.* Grand Rapids, MI: Zondervan Publishing House.

71. Wilkins, Michael J. 1992. *Following the Master: discipleship in the steps of Jesus*. Grand Rapids, MI: Zondervan Publishing House.

HOW YOU CAN HAVE
A RELATIONSHIP WITH JESUS

✓ GOD LOVES YOU AND HAS A WONDERFUL PLAN FOR YOUR LIFE

For I know the plans I have for you," declares the LORD, "plans to prosper you and not to harm you, plans to give you hope and a future. **Jeremiah 29:11 (NIV)**

✓ AS A RESULT OF MAN GOING HIS OWN WAY AND REJECTING GOD, A CHASM, A GREAT DIVIDE, HAS COME SEPARATING A JUST AND HOLY GOD FROM SINFUL MAN

for all have sinned and fall short of the glory of God, **Romans 3:23 (NIV)**

For the wages of sin is death, but the gift of God is eternal life in Christ Jesus our Lord. **Romans 6:23 (NIV)**

✓ GOD SENT HIS SON, HIS PERFECT SON TO BECOME OUR SACRIFICE. HE WHO IS SINLESS TOOK UPON HIMSELF OUR SINS, OFFERING TO RESTORE OUR BROKEN RELATIONSHIP WITH GOD, BRIDGING THE GAP BETWEEN GOD AND MAN

We all, like sheep, have gone astray, each of us has turned to his own way; and the LORD has laid on him the iniquity of us all. **Isaiah 53:6 (NIV)**

The next day John saw Jesus coming toward him and said, "Look, the Lamb of God, who takes away the sin of the world!" **John 1:29 (NIV)**

✓ GOD HAS GIVEN EACH MAN A CHOICE EITHER TO ACCEPT THE FREE GIFT OF SALVATION AND LIVE FOREVER OR TO REJECT HIS GRACIOUS GIFT AND SPEND ETERNITY FOREVER SEPARATED FROM GOD

For God so loved the world that he gave his one and only Son, that whoever believes in him shall not perish but have eternal life. **John 3:16 (NIV)**

[12]Yet to all who received him, to those who believed in his name, he gave the right to become children of God-- [13]children born not of natural descent, nor of human decision or a husband's will, but born of God. **John 1:12-13 (NIV)**

Essential Spiritual Growth Resources from
Something New Christian Publishers
and Quality Leadership Consultants

Websites, Newsletter, and Blogs:

www.dennybates.com and www.ReallyGoodDay4U.com is the hub for all of our teaching and coaching resources. Check out our free downloads as well as our store.

www.thequalitydisciple.com links to dennybates.com.

www.qualityleadershipconsultants.com links to dennybates.com.

www.thequalitydisciple.blogspot.com is the teaching blog for Psalms of Discipleship.

www.facebook.com/denny.bates is my portal to social networking.

Dr. Denny Bates and Quality Leadership Tips For You is my newsletter. Featured leadership articles, devotional thoughts, and a menu of coaching and book resources.

Sign up at http://www.dennybates.com

Books:

Other titles from the Quality Discipleship Series:

- ❖ How To Study And Apply The Bible To Your Life (PDF Book only)
- ❖ Growing Up…Practical Bible Studies For New And Growing Christians (PDF Book only)
- ❖ Psalms of Discipleship: A One Year Journey With The Shepherd (Kindle or printed copy)
- ❖ Christmas Meditations of Worship: Four Weeks of Advent (Kindle or printed copy)
- ❖ Living Above The Fray: Learning The Seven Healthy Leadership Principles That Will Shelter You From The Destructive Effects Of Leader-I-Tis (Kindle or printed copy)
- ❖ My Spiritual Life Plan: Creating An Effective Spiritual Life Plan For The Quality Disciple (Kindle or printed copy)
- ❖ Living Above The Fray Leadership Assessment: The Coaches Guide For Leading With Quality In Mind (Kindle or printed copy)
- ❖ Building A Christian Community Of Friends: Four Practical Studies On Biblical Friendships (Kindle or printed copy)
- ❖ Changing Places: Understanding The Process Of Transition. (Kindle or printed copy)
- ❖ Life-Ol-Ogy: Mastering The Study Of Your Life, Your Team, Your Profession and Your Customers (Kindle or printed copy)
- ❖ Growing In Greatness: *31 Living Legacy Principles From the Proverbs For the Quality Leader (Proverbs 1:1-5:14), Volume 1* (Kindle or printed copy)
- ❖ Quality Wisdom For A Modern Age: The Wisdom Book Of Proverbs (Kindle or printed copy)
- ❖ How To Have A Really Good Day With The GOS-PILL During Times Of Crisis: 31 Days Of Inspiration (Kindle or printed copy)
- ❖ The Fine Art Of Experiencing Quality Relationships: 31 Intentional Days Of Thoughtful Treasures From Proverbs That Will Transform The Heart (Kindle or printed copy)
- ❖ How To Build A Better Business By The Proverbs: 31 Intentional Days Of Best Practices That Will Lead To Your Success (Kindle or printed copy)
- ❖ Bitter Busters: How Bitter Busters Can Set You Free From Becoming Bitter Against Family, Friends, Career, Church and God." (Kindle or printed copy)

Retreat Journals:

- ❖ The Power – Broker's Guide To The Kingdom
- ❖ Four Legacies For A Life Change
- ❖ Three Commitments That Change A Life
- ❖ Growing In Grace: A Fresh Look At Biblical Discipleship
- ❖ Adding Quality To Your Life

Contact us for availability and cost. www.dennybates.com

Help Me Write My Story Books (A ghost writing and book coaching custom service)

For information see the next page or connect to **www.HelpMeWriteMyStory.com**

Here are a few of my Help Me Write My Story clients. Please check them out on Amazon.

- ❖ "Touched by Him: A Man Who Said Yes To Jesus" by Harry F. Lyles as told to Dr. Denny Bates (Something New Christian Publishers)
- ❖ "I'm Just Rebeckah Wilhelmina And I Found A Way Out" by Rebeckah Wilhelmina (Healthy Curves Count Publishers)
- ❖ "The Blue Duck: Learning How To Discover Your Competitive Edge And Celebrate The Uniqueness Of You" by Sandra Mason (Younique Publishers)
- ❖ "How To Kick Your Own Butt: The Fine Art Of Leading Yourself Well" by Carol Mabe (CMC Transformational Publishing)
- ❖ "My Life: Then And Now: Won't He Do It" by Karen Calhoun (KMJC Publishers)
- ❖ "More Than A Seed: The Yearn For God's Children To Accept, Grow, And Fight" by Akayla Frazier (Changed Legacy Publishing)
- ❖ "Life-Sustaining Hope" by Dr. Patrick Hunt (M2E Motivational Consulting)
- ❖ "How The Puppy Learned To Cherish Life by Dr. Patrick Hunt (M2E Motivational Consulting)
- ❖ "My Miscarriage: And Other Uninvited Events" by Traci McCombs (Skinny Brown Dog Media)
- ❖ "Take the Soap" by Bryan Braddock, Byon "kNOw Ca$h" McCullough as told to Dr. Denny Bates (Take The Soap Publishers—TBA)

What is your story?

Help Me Write My Story (HMWMS)
www.HelpMeWriteMyStory.com

HELP ME WRITE MY STORY is a highly relational, process-driven, professional service that empowers an aspiring author to produce a personal memoir that is shared in a self-published book (including Kindle too). HELP ME WRITE MY STORY helps you to focus on this acrostic:

H = **Heartfelt** (The best place to begin writing your story is in the HEART)

M = **Memories** (If you do not WRITE THEM DOWN you will eventually FORGET many of them)

W = **Well-spoken** (To tell your story you've got to be a CLEAR COMMUNICATOR so you will be understood)

M = **Motivational** (It's important for you not to only share with your readers how CHALLENGING your circumstances may have been but it's even more important to share how you faced your obstacles and got through them SUCCESSFULLY)

S = **Strategic** (Your story will most likely not speak to everyone, but it will speak to SOMEONE, so it's important to know WHO you are seeking to influence the most and why)

I believe that our lives are the sum of many stories filled with adventures, wonders, disappointments, successes, tragedies, victories, and mysteries. Our **STORIES**, all of them, have the necessary components for a lasting legacy.

Your story is a **GIFT** to others. Your life is a **STEWARDSHIP**. Your story matters because **YOU MATTER**. Your story needs to be **SHARED** with and **REMEMBERED** by those who need to KNOW your story.
That said, many **STORIES** never go beyond the back of our minds and fade away forever. And that is why I am writing to you. I want to help you **WRITE YOUR STORY**.

IMAGINE for a moment what you could do with **YOUR STORY** in the **FORM** of a **BOOK**:

- **YOUR STORY**, in the form of a quality published book, becomes something tangible and is in your hands.

- **YOUR STORY** can give encouragement to others, especially to your family, friends, and customers/clients, and even to people you will unlikely ever meet in this life.

56

- **YOUR STORY** contains your legacy and will always be there, even after you are long gone, influencing future readers.

- **YOUR STORY**, in the form of a book, will be the perfect and unique item for you to give away or sell, creating a new revenue stream.

- **YOUR STORY** can serve as a mentor to help the person who wants to learn how to apply the life lessons you experienced.

YOUR STORY matters to you and **YOUR STORY** matters to me too.

What is HELP ME WRITE MY STORY?

HELP ME WRITE MY STORY coaches the author / client through each creative phase of writing a book:

- How to create the Big Story Idea
- How to create a *Write My Story Time Line*
- How to do great research
- How to create a strong outline of chapters and subchapters
- How to use creative words to paint vivid mental and emotional images
- How to tell your story in an interesting way
- How to write strong chapter summaries
- How to create of book title and subtitle that resonates with the reader
- How to create a book front and back cover that catches the reader's attention
- How to write back cover copy
- How to take an author's story to the finished product in print and in Kindle formats.
- How to use the power of social networking to promote your story

Who needs HELP ME WRITE MY STORY?

HELP ME WRITE MY STORY can be a great resource for the person who . . .

- Wants to write their story but needs practical instruction, intentional coaching and accountability.

- Wants to make sure their story and their legacy is preserved in a format so family members and friends will remember and be inspired.

- Wants to use their story as a way to open doors for future opportunities for even greater influence.

- Wants a personal product to either sell or gift to others.

- Wants the rewarding satisfaction of having a professional copy of their personal story.

How does HELP ME WRITE MY STORY work?

Each writing project has its own unique set of challenges, but I've sought to present three different packages and pricing levels. All five are dependent upon the pace, progress, and extraordinary challenges of the book.

There are five Story Coaching service levels of Help Me Write My Story*:

In addition to the fees for each package, a reduced monthly payment plus a percentage of the royalties is an alternative form of payment. Ask Dr. Bates for the details.

Help Me Write My Story Books is a ghost writing and book coaching custom service.

For information connect to **www.HelpMeWriteMyStory.com**

QUALITY LEADERSHIP CONSULTANTS

PROFESSIONAL COACHING, CONSULTING,
AND TEACHING
Presenting Quality Ideas;
Producing Quality Leaders

Introducing Dr. Denny Bates
Professional Life, Business Coach, Teacher, Writer, Speaker And Consultant

Why is it important for you to have a professional quality life coach and leadership trainer?

It has been said, "Experience is the best guide in life." The truth is *guided experience* is the best guide! Time, money, and emotional energy can be saved by linking up with a person who already understands where you are, where you want to go and has a good grasp on how to lead you there in a positive way.

What kind of guided experience do I offer?

Seasoned in both the marketplace and non-profit settings, I can offer you and/or your organization Quality Leadership coaching tracks with a relational emphasis. For instance: Personal Growth, Communication Skills, Building Healthy Relationships, Career Counseling / Job Performance, Life Transitions, Organizational Health; and for faith-based individuals and/or organizations, Spiritual Growth. My practical experience in both for-profit and non-profit settings, coupled with my academic and professional training, affords me the ability to offer you unique Quality Leadership services.

The JOHN MAXWELL **Team**

AN INDEPENDENT CERTIFIED COACH, TEACHER AND SPEAKER
WITH THE JOHN MAXWELL TEAM

My friend John Maxwell says,

"Everything rises and falls on leadership"

As a Leadership Specialist,
I can help YOU in the marketplace!

✓ With years of experience working as a manager in the marketplace, I know what it takes to create a healthy organization. I can train your leaders and employees in effective teamwork and communication.

✓ I know how to help business leaders practice the kind of self-care that not only benefits them personally, but also adds value to the company.

✓ I know how to help a management team build a culture that places great value on integrity and success.

✓ I can help you and your leaders set reasonable goals and show you the tools to help you reach each one.

✓ I can help you reproduce your values, vision and passion in the lives of others.

✓ I can help you sharpen your leadership skills in a group coaching setting or one to one. As a professional life coach and leadership trainer, I can offer you the finest coaching and training resources available today as a certified coach, teacher and speaker for the John Maxwell Team.

QUALITY
LEADERSHIP CONSULTANTS
Email dennybates@gmail.com
www.dennybates.com

What does a Disciple-Making Ministry look like?
It looks like . . .

SOMETHING *new*

"Do not call to mind the former things, or ponder things of the past; Behold, I will do something new . . ." Isaiah 43:18, 19a

- A ministry that focuses upon making Quality disciples for Jesus

- A ministry that encourages believers to connect in community and experience the discipled life

- A ministry that seeks to help a body of believers to learn how to live the discipled life through seminars, workshops, keynote speaking and interactive coaching

Contact Dr. Denny Bates for more information on how you and your church can create a culture of DiscipleMakers4Jesus

www.TheQualityDisciple.com

What Others Are Saying About My Leadership Coaching And Discipleship Via DiscipleMakers4Jesus (DM4J)

I know and have worked with Denny Bates for more than a decade. Denny now serves as a leadership trainer and coach. It is my pleasure to recommend Denny as a valuable and trusted resource for leadership training and coaching. In addition to earning his doctoral degree in leadership, Denny is also an independent certified coach, teacher, and speaker for The John Maxwell Team. I believe you and your organization will benefit from his knowledge of what leaders need in order to grow as a leader. You will appreciate Denny's relational approach to leadership training and his ability to connect with people. Dr. Bates offers workshops, seminars, keynote speaking, and coaching ... aiding your personal and professional growth through study and practical application of John Maxwell's leadership methods. **(President and CEO of Regional Hospital)**

Just wanted to let you know how much our time of coaching and leadership development has meant to me. Every time I am faced with a challenge I try to walk thru the Grace tree of wisdom. You set the example every day of the man of God I want to be. Thank you! **(Corporate Manager of Medical Services)**

[I've learned] to keep the main thing the main thing!! To take care of the people that God puts in front of me everyday. **(Sales Manager of automotive dealership)**

Denny has been my friend, pastor, colleague, mentor and confidant for almost 10 years. During this time, Denny has led me through tough waters, given me wise counsel and taught me practical ways to live out my faith while falling more in love with my Savior. **(Youth Pastor)**

Other than my own father, Denny has been my most trusted friend and spiritual mentor. Denny's discipleship has been truly transforming and helped me to realize the importance of investing in others as he has invested in me. **(Medical Device Consultant)**

I treasure my relationship with Denny because we share a common heart to help people discover all that Christ wants to do in and through them. **(Disciple-Making Missionary to Eastern Europe)**

I have known Denny for many years and have had the privilege to work with him on the same pastoral staff for over 5 years. During that time I have sought Denny's counsel on many issues ranging from personal struggles to theological questions. Denny has always provided me with poignant, gracious and thoughtful counsel. They say that everyone should have a mentor and I am blessed to be able to consider Denny my mentor. He has been an invaluable asset in my life and ministry. **(Clinical Counselor)**

My relationship with Denny has been personal, honest, and Christ-centered. Denny's common sense approach to the issues of life is always soundly based on scriptural principles. I remember discussing with Denny how I felt that I needed to do so much service for the Lord because of all the times I had failed Him. Denny gently said to me, "It's all about grace". I was reminded that there is no 'payback' plan for the Lord. **(Pastor)**

Having a group of peers who candidly discuss the awesome responsibility that each carries as a servant and hearing how God has responded so richly to our needs clearly demonstrates how marvelous is our God, who works in each of our lives to do His will. **(Hospital Vice-President in a discipleship group for executives)**

Denny and I have know each other for nearly fifteen years, we bonded shortly after he had his heart attack because of an illness I had years prior – Guillain-Barre Syndrome – that made me more aware of the right priorities I should have in life. Through this episode and having children similar in age we bonded in a unique and special way rarely achieved between men. Approximately one year ago I lost my job as a senior executive at a large international company that I had been with 26 years, during the transition period of me finding another job Denny was an extreme encouragement to me. During a time when I was wrestling between accepting a position or not and I will never forget what Denny told me "You can just accept it as God's providential care". He was right! I later humbly accepted the position as President & Chief Operating Officer for a Subsea Oilfield Manufacturing company. **(Corporate Executive)**

Denny has been a teacher / mentor / discipler / encourager / prayer partner and great friend who God has used to help me keep a godly perspective on the different times & issues of life I've gone through as I've seek to follow Jesus. Once while praying with Denny through a career move, he encouraged me to think of the gifts & skills I had and then ask what I had a passion for, and then to ask God to show me how they can fit together. From this I learned to stop putting these gifts & skills in a "Box" and limiting what God could do with them, and use them for. For the first time, as I now work for a non-profit Christian organization as a warehouse manager, I feel I'm using the gifts and abilities God has given me to fulfill His purpose at something I really have a passion for! **(Former market place worker, now Missionary who is impacting the world)**

Denny met with me at 7 a.m. every Friday for a year. He came to me knowing he would receive my weekly burdens. This is not the way any of us would choose to begin our day. He does not judge nor do I ever feel judged. He is one of the most selfless and giving person I have ever met. This is easy to say because I know he is just a man. His obedience to God sets him apart. He taught me to live by grace, be long suffering, and love my wife regardless of my excuses. **(Medical Worker, Physical therapist assistant)**

Through a lifestyle of disciple making, Denny Bates has shown me what it truly means to live out Matthew 28: 19, 20. **(Educator)**

I've heard it said that on this side of eternity that there are only two things that you can be certain of: death and taxes. I'm certain of three things; the first two and that I have a friend in Denny Bates! I asked God at the beginning of my ministry to bring solid men into my life that would disciple me, teach me and hold me accountable. Denny has been an extreme answer to that prayer. **(Church-planting Pastor)**

Dr. Denny Bates opened my eyes to the power of small groups. He showed me what a true mentor really is. I will be forever grateful for his leadership, friendship, and love! **(Videographer)**

Practical application of God's teachings by normal, everyday family men such as myself; that's what DM4J means to me. Listening to and sharing the innumerable ways the Lord touches the lives of each and every man in this group is not only uplifting, but inspiring. From the greatest trials to what might seem trivial, God has a plan and a purpose for it all. The value of DM4J to me is immeasurable. **(Pharmacist)**

About Dr. Denny Bates

Dr. Denny Bates is Principal Consultant for Quality Leadership Consultants, founder of Something New Christian Publishers, Something New Ministries and The Quality Disciple, Life Coach for iHope Christian Care and Counseling, adjunct faculty mentor in the Columbia Biblical Seminary online Doctor of Ministerial Leadership program, and a founding member of the John Maxwell Team of certified coaches, speakers, and trainers. He has earned degrees from Francis Marion College [B.S.] and Columbia Biblical Seminary and School of Missions [MDiv, DMin]. With a doctoral degree in personal and organizational leadership, he is well equipped to serve as teacher, life coach, mentor, disciplemaker, motivational speaker and writer for his own leadership and personal growth titles as well as helping others write their stories*

Denny has written for an international publisher of Bible commentary, served as the Discipleship Pastor in the local church, as well as being a leader in the marketplace by creating the social networking brand #Aisle31. By God's grace, he seeks to live above the fray and "Press on!" Visit **www.dennybates.com**.

*See www.HelpMeWriteMyStory.com for this custom service.

About iHope Christian Care And Counseling

MISSION STATEMENT:

To bring hope and healing to the community through professional counseling and care rooted in biblical principles.

The vision of iHope Christian Care and Counseling, Inc. is to be a distinctly Christian counseling center serving individuals, families, couples, and ministry leaders with affordable counseling and care. We are committed to offering hope and healing through Jesus Christ. As Christian counselors, we are called to bind up the brokenhearted, proclaim freedom for the captive, and comfort those who mourn. iHope desires to be an extender of the local church, offering counsel to those going through a season of difficulty. We are a support and resource for local pastors and for our community. Many people desire counseling and healing offered through Jesus Christ, but they do not know where to turn, cannot afford counseling, or are unaware of available resources. iHope is intended to be a resource within reach of anyone who wants help.

CORE VALUES

iHope operates by five core values. These values guide our counseling work, education, and interactions with the community and are grounded in Scripture.

- **Christ-centered**
  Remain consistently true to the Gospel of Jesus Christ and his Word in Scripture
  John 15:1-8

- **Kingdom-minded**
  Engage with the local church to care for and connect clients to the body of Christ
  Acts 2:42-47, Romans 12:4-5

- **Ethics, Integrity, and Excellence**
  Maintain the ethical standards of the American Association of Christian Counselors, practicing with integrity and competency
  Proverbs 11:3, Proverbs 28:6, 1 Peter 3:16

- **Accessibility**
  Be a resource within reach of anyone who needs help.
  Philippians 2:5-8, Galatians 6:2, Proverbs 22:9

- **Whole-Person Care**
  Serve and care for each person's holistic health — spiritual, mental, relational, physical, and emotional health and wellness.
  Matthew 22:36-39, Matthew 14:14-21

www.ReallyGoodDay4U.com

https://ihopeflorence.com

Praise For Bitter Busters:

Denny teaches us in this book that a bitter spirit can happen to any of us if we aren't careful. Anything from unresolved anger, unforgiving attitudes, resentment, jealousy, disappointment are just some of life's struggles that cause us to plunge us into bitterness. We must hold God close to our hearts and learn the Word of God to overtake and bust our bitterness. We must come back to our Lord when bitterness overtakes our hearts.

"I have told you these things, so that in me you may have peace. In this world you will have trouble. But take heart! I have overcome the world." Thank you to my Lord and Denny for busting my bitterness♥

Kim Lanier, BSN, RN
Director of Heart and Vascular Day Hospital & Recovery
Director of Cardiac and Pulmonary Rehabilitation

As a woman who experienced infertility, miscarriages, cancer, and what so many refer to as "daddy issues," I can honestly say I wish I had Bitter Busters years ago. Denny not only opens up about his own experience with bitterness, but he also provides biblically sound examples and practices we can use to help us fight past unforgiveness and anger. This book is an excellent reminder that busting out of bitterness is a process and that God is with us every step of the way.

Traci McCombs, MBA
Author of #1 Amazon Best Seller, *My Miscarriages: And Other Uninvited Events*

Bitter Busters engages with the natural desire of human bitterness in particular situations with practical principles to avoid or overcome bitterness. During times of rejection, it is our hearts default to become bitter with the person or situation. However, living a Christ filled life as depicted in *Bitter Busters* gives one strength to live an intentional life to choose love to destroy the desire to become bitter.

Dr. Marlo D. Brayboy
Columbia International University

Dr. Bates's book Bitter Busters has called me to reflect on issues I have "swept under the rug" for quite some time relating to my own family, friends, church, work, and relationship with God. Our world's mentality, since our fall as humans in the Garden of Eden, has been not to forgive but get even when wronged and become bitter when we are treated unfairly by others. Dr. Bates's book is biblically sound and teaches us God's love and presence in our lives is the only way to overcome what comes naturally. The book is loaded with scriptural references to equip us as Christians to help root out and prevent bitterness from destroying our personal life, lives of others, but most importantly our relationship with God. Thank you Dr. Bates for sharing your personal experiences and life lessons with us along with the Biblical solution to this sin so prevalent in our world and society today!

Stephen M. Welch.,BS, MAT
Science Educator

Bitter Busters is a go-to resource for anyone who has experienced hurt in their life. Through excellent Bible teaching, real life examples and authentic stories Denny guides the reader towards a path of healing from the pain of broken relationships. I cannot more highly recommend this book as a go-to guide for leading you away from the prison of bitterness and unforgiveness and towards the path of freedom, peace and healing.

F. Reeves Cannon, III, M.A.,LPC, BCPCC
Executive Pastor, Church at Sandhurst

We all can and have been guilty of embracing bitterness – someone has done something, said something, that hurt us deeply. We are fallen people living in a fallen world and for Christ followers, this is especially onerous. The root of bitterness is like a *root bearing poisonous fruit* (Deut 29:18). So, what do we do? In his book, Denny has presented a Scripture based process for busting free from bitterness. Scriptural examples paired with practical personal application, provide freedom, refreshment, and restoration. I have watched Denny live it. A thorough Subject Index is included making this a valuable reference source.

Ron Bennett
Church Elder

Dr. Denny Bates has created a wonderful guidebook for dealing with the difficult times of life without becoming bitter. Moreover, he points past bitterness to a fulfilled life of compassion and love. Furthermore, his rich life of serving others bears witness to the truth of his testimonies.

Dr. Patrick Hunt – *Author of the Pathway of Happiness: Cherish Life and Live Nobly.*

Forgiveness…are you kidding me! Denny has taken on a most difficult topic that reaches into the lives of us all. We aren't built for it in our own power. So why read Bitter Busters? In it is the prescription for not only why to forgive, but how to make it your reality. As someone who has, personally, lived out the necessity for both self and other forgiveness, I believe Denny has done an excellent job of combining the scriptures to unlock the powerful antidote to our natural, human response of bitterness. Bitter Busters is an easy to read resource which guides us to the Truth that Forgiveness really is a gift that we should want to give to ourselves. Thank you Denny, for this work; I pray that in it many will discover His Truth, and through Him find their Freedom.

Leslie Rutten
Homemaker/Occupational Therapist

Denny, we have read your new book Bitter Busters and very impressed with it. You have expressed well your hurts and disappointments, yet our God has led you into a place of acceptance and forgiveness. Now you have shared the scriptural examples of how God, in His faithfulness, has given you His grace and love. May God use it mightily to help others.
Love,
Gail & Harry Lyles
Author of *Touched By Him: A Man Who Said Yes To Jesus*

Denny has written this from his heart. In my opinion, he is the perfect one to have penned this as I know he lives out what he writes. Thanks for reminding me that forgiveness and busting bitterness go hand in hand and that God is the authority that not only commands and enables us to do it, but also exemplifies it to us through Jesus. Well done, Denny.

Sandy Richardson
Owner, Morningstar Farms

Bitter Busters is a must read for anyone who has ever gone through any hardship or trauma and has difficulty letting go of the bitterness of betrayal. No doubt life is hard but having bitterness as a constant companion makes living even more difficult. This book gives a new way of dealing with the bitterness in a way that gives God the glory and allows the captives to bitterness be set free! Denny has a unique way of weaving his real-life story with God's truth and providing a way out of the bitterness through what is now known as Bitter Busters! This book will change your life and bring a renewed sense of wholeness that can only be experienced through inner healing and forgiveness. May you be set free from bitterness by using the God-given principles outlined in this Masterpiece called Bitter Busters.

Kimberly Eaker MSN, APRN, FNP-C
Nurse Practitioner, Department of Defense

Praise For The Intimate Journey To Desires:

I'm honored that you asked me to read it. I can't imagine the time you've poured into this work, especially with the indexes at the back. Whoever gave you that wise counsel was onto something. It certainly does take it to the next level! Wonderful! The content was clear as you described each level of intimacy. I did find myself thinking, "Ok but HOW do I take the next step?" And then you showed the reader how in the next section. You answered my question!

The way you explore each area up against the scriptures brings a level of trust and confidence, like sure footing for the journey. Through comparison of the assessment sections the reader is able to get a sense of where they are strong and where they are lacking. Each is followed up with steady encouragement and a "how to" next step . . . We all desire intimacy and the work to achieve it is never easy. But it extends to our deepest needs and for that we will work! Whether we're single, dating, or in a marriage, our relationship with Jesus is at the core of who we are and who we are able to be for others. It feels good to hit the sweet spot, and we can! Being proactive and using this roadmap give us a healthy journey to travel. You've given me a nudge in the right direction. I'm in! Thank you for sharing this with me. I'm considering it a gift and once you publish, I'll share it with others. You are truly a disciple maker!

Blessings,
Erika Miller, LPC

In *The Intimate Journey To Desires*, Dr. Denny Bates does a masterful job of laying a foundation of God and His completeness as the Holy Trinity and then moves to His desire for intimacy with His creation. God desires that we grow into all that He desires for us and Dr. Bates outlines a solid road-map on how we, through Biblical spiritual disciplines, can find that relationship with God. The flow of this work leads us on a journey to realize that, once we have that relationship with God in the proper place in our lives, only then can we know the fullness of relationships with others. Dr. Bates clearly shows us how to find that "Sweet Spot" on the journey to discovering God's best for us. Dr. Bates' heart for God and for his fellow believers is clear and genuine, and this book will make a difference for every believer!!!!!

Dr. David Wike
Lead Pastor, Ebeneezer Baptist Church

Denny has been a true friend for many years. God has blessed him with the spiritual gift of encouragement, among many other gifts. He uses it in such incredible ways through which Aubrey and I have personally experienced. Whether it be the spoken word, the written word or his genuine countenance, you always go away changed! Denny has such a heartfelt desire to bring others to the place God has called them to be. Knowing when they are in that place, they are free to "Be." He values each person he meets and gives them great worth in the beautiful God has called them to be.

This book, *The Intimate Journey To Desires*, has masterfully taken the scripture to simplify them to cause us to desire intimacy with God, family and countless others. It has refreshed our spirit and refreshed our love for our dear Brother in Christ, Denny, as our tour guide.

Debbie and Aubrey Phipps
Ephesians 3:20

He has a Kingdom purpose for my life. As I spend time getting to know Him more intimately, I will be able to hear His voice. One of the best words in my vocabulary these days is authenticity. It is absolutely necessary for healthy relationships. Who better to practice authenticity, complete emotional and spiritual exposure, the real me (us) with than the One who knows us completely already? . . . Intimacy is so difficult to understand much less display. I think it takes a good long look at those who have hurt us as well as those we can truly say love us. It is hard to trust an unseen God with our scarred hearts. When I give God my undivided attention in worship...reading His Word, praying, singing His praises, stilling my heart. I can't help but to see Him.

Helen Dobbins Rogers, RN

The Intimate Journey To Desires

God's Best For You! (For Any Meaningful Relationships)

"Don't Settle For Less, Than God's Best!"

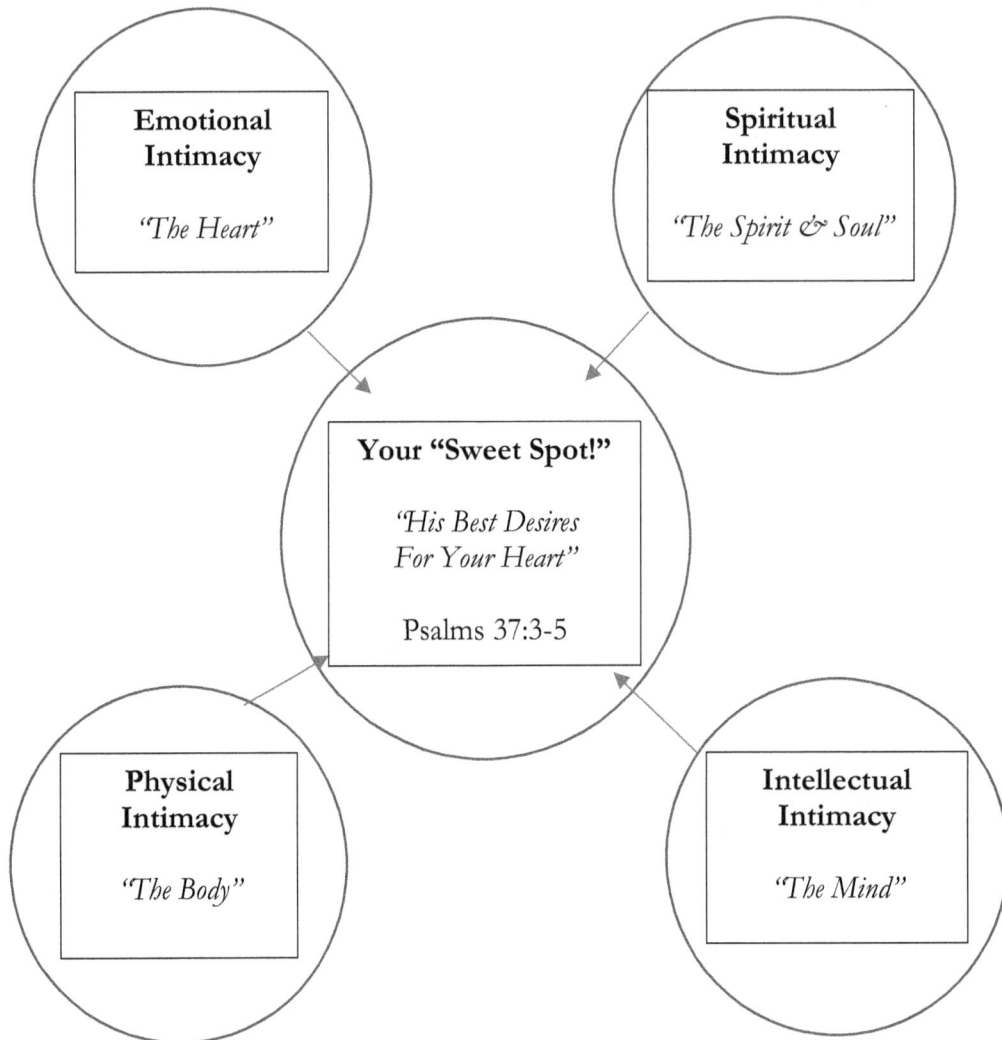

Emotional Intimacy

"The Heart"

Spiritual Intimacy

"The Spirit & Soul"

Your "Sweet Spot!"

"His Best Desires For Your Heart"

Psalms 37:3-5

Physical Intimacy

"The Body"

Intellectual Intimacy

"The Mind"

Intimate Journey To Desires

©2022 Dr. Denny Bates & Something New Ministries